Aristotle. A Quick Immersion

Quick Immersions uses accurate and straightforward language to offer a good introduction, or deeper knowledge, on diverse issues, as well-structured texts by prestigious authors delve into the worlds of political and social sciences, philosophy, science and the humanities.

C. D. C. Reeve

ARISTOTLE

A Quick Immersion

Tibidabo Publishing
New York

Published by Tibidabo Publishing, Inc.

Cover art by Raimon Guirado

First published 2019

Visit our Series on our Web:
www.quickimmersions.com

ISBN: 978-1-949845-08-2
3 4 5 6 7 8 9 10

Printed in the United States of America.

Contents

Abbreviations

Citations of Aristotle's works are standardly made to Immanuel Bekker, *Aristotelis Opera* (Berlin: De Gruyter, 1831 [1970]), in the canonical form of abbreviated title (omitted when unneeded), column letter ([a] or [b]), and line number. An * indicates a work whose authenticity has been seriously questioned, ** indicates a work attributed to Aristotle but generally agreed not to be by him. The abbreviations used are as follows:

APo.	*Posterior Analytics*
APr.	*Prior Analytics*
Cael.	*De Caelo (On the Heavens)*
Cat.	*Categories*
DA	*De Anima (On the Soul)*
Div. Somn.	*On Divination in Sleep*
EE	*Eudemian Ethics*
GA	*Generation of Animals*
GC	*On Coming to Be and Passing Away*
HA	*History of Animals*
Insomn.	*On Dreams*
Juv.	*On Youth and Old Age, Life and Death, and Respiration*
MA	*Movement of Animals*
MM	*Magna Moralia**
Mem.	*On Memory*
Met.	*Metaphysics*
Mete.	*Meteorology*
Mu.	*De Mundo***
NE	*Nicomachean Ethics*
PA	*Parts of Animals*

Ph.	*Physics*
Po.	*Poetics*
Pol.	*Politics*
Protr.	*Protrepticus*
Rh.	*Rhetoric*
Sens.	*De Sensu*
Somn.	*On Sleep*
Top.	*Topics*

English translations of these works are available in Jonathan Barnes, *The Complete Works of Aristotle: The Revised Oxford Translation* (Princeton: Princeton University Press, 1984). Many of the most important and widely read are also available in my own uniform annotated translations in the *New Hackett Aristotle Series* from Hackett Publishing Company (Cambridge, Indianapolis), which are the ones used in this book:

Aristotle: Physics (2018)
Aristotle: De Caelo (2020)
Aristotle: On Coming to Be and Passing Away & Meteorology IV (2020)
Aristotle: De Anima (2017)
Aristotle: Generation of Animals & History of Animals I, Parts of Animals I (2019)
Aristotle: Metaphysics (2016)
Aristotle: Nicomachean Ethics (2014)
Aristotle: Politics A New Translation (2017)
Aristotle: Rhetoric (2018)

Chapter 1

Life and Works

Aristotle was born in 384 BC to a well-off family living in the small town of Stagira in northern Greece. His father, Nicomachus, who died while Aristotle was still quite young, was allegedly doctor to King Amyntas of Macedon. His mother, Phaestis, was wealthy in her own right. When Aristotle was seventeen his guardian, Proxenus, sent him to study at Plato's Academy in Athens. He remained there for twenty years, initially as a student, eventually as a researcher and teacher.

When Plato died in 347, leaving the Academy in the hands of his nephew Speusippus, Aristotle left Athens for Assos in Asia Minor, where the ruler,

Hermias, was a patron of philosophy. He married Hermias' niece (or ward) Pythias, and had a daughter by her, also named Pythias. Three years later, in 345, after Hermias had been killed by the Persians, Aristotle moved to Mytilene on the island of Lesbos, where he met Theophrastus, who was to become his best student and closest colleague.

In 343 Aristotle seems to have been invited by Philip of Macedon to be tutor to the latter's thirteen-year-old son, Alexander, later called "the Great." In 335 Aristotle returned to Athens and founded his own institute, the Lyceum. While he was there his wife died and he established a relationship with Herpyllis, also a native of Stagira. Their son Nicomachus was named for Aristotle's father, and the *Nicomachean Ethics* may, in turn, have been named for him or transcribed by him. In 323 Alexander the Great died, with the result that anti-Macedonian feeling in Athens grew stronger. Perhaps threatened with a formal charge of impiety (*NE* $1177^{b}33$), Aristotle left for Chalcis in Euboea, where he died twelve months later, in 322, at the age of sixty-two.

Legend has it that Aristotle had slender calves, small eyes, spoke with a lisp, and was "conspicuous by his attire, his rings, and the cut of his hair." His will reveals that he had a sizable estate, a domestic partner, two children, a considerable library, and a large circle of friends. In it Aristotle asks his executors to take special care of Herpyllis. He directs that his slaves be freed "when they come of age" and that the bones of his wife, Pythias, be mixed with his "as she instructed."

The surviving writings of Aristotle

Although the surviving writings of Aristotle occupy almost 2,500 tightly printed pages in English, most of them are not works polished for publication but sometimes incomplete lecture notes and working papers. This accounts for some, though not all, of their legendary difficulty. It is unfair to complain, as a Platonist opponent did, that Aristotle "escapes refutation by clothing a perplexing subject in obscure language, using darkness like a squid to make himself hard to catch," but there is darkness and obscurity enough for anyone, even if none of it is intentional. There is also a staggering breadth and depth of intellect. Aristotle made fundamental contributions to a vast range of disciplines, as the list of his surviving writings indicates, including logic, metaphysics, epistemology, psychology, ethics, politics, rhetoric, aesthetics, zoology, biology, physics, and philosophical and political history. When Dante called him "the master of those who know," he was scarcely exaggerating.

Precisely because of the depth and breadth of his thought, however, and the nature of his writings as we have them, Aristotle requires and most rewards a resolute and persistent reader. The present book, like others in the series, is intended as a guide for well-informed but non-specialist readers; but it too requires some resolution and persistence. For an immersion—even a quick one—in so complex a thinker cannot do its job unless it plumbs those depths. Hence much of what you are about to read takes the form of close readings of pieces of Aristotle's own writings, to give you the feel for what it is like to read them, and also to give you first-hand evidence for the views I argue they contain. Aristotle would be happy with nothing less.

Chapter 2

Matter and Form

According to Aristotle we find in nature an apparently continuous scale of beings, in which, for example, animate beings—beings with souls—differ only very slightly from inanimate ones in their level of formation:

> Nature proceeds from the inanimate to the animals by such small steps that, because of the continuity, we fail to see to which the boundary and the middle between them belongs. For the first genus of thing after the inanimate is the plant genus, and, among these, one differs from another in seeming to have a greater share of life; but the whole genus, in comparison with the other inanimate bodies,

> appears almost as animate, while in comparison with the animal genus it appears inanimate. The change from plants to animals is continuous, as we said before. (*HA* 588[b]4–12)

The sublunary elements (earth, water, air, and fire) aside, the simplest beings on this scale are homoeomerous or uniform stuffs, such as wood, olive oil, flesh, and bone, whose parts have the same account as the whole (*GC* 314[a]20). These are constituted out of the elements in some ratio, when the active capacities (hot, cold) in the elements master the corresponding passive ones (dry, wet):

> Having determined these things, we must grasp the workings of these, namely, the workings of the ones capable of affecting, and the species of the affectable ones. First off, then, universally [speaking], unconditional coming to be and natural change is the function of these capacities, as is the opposite passing away that is in accord with nature. And these processes occur both in plants and in animals and their parts. Unconditional and natural coming to be is a change due to these capacities—when they stand in the right ratio (*logos*)—in the matter that by nature underlies a given thing, this being the capacities to be affected that we have just mentioned. When the hot and the cold master the matter they cause coming to be. (*Mete.* 378[b]26–379[a]1)

The fundamental form of such mastery is concoction (*pepsis*), which is responsible for producing a uniform stuff, and for preserving its nature thereafter:

> Concoction, then, is a completion due to the natural and proper heat that comes from the underlying affectable things, these being the matter proper to the given thing. For when it has been concocted it is completed and has come to be. And the starting-point of the completion comes about due to the proper heat, even if certain external aids helped to accomplish it—for example, nourishment is helped to concoct even due to baths and due to other things of this sort. And the end in some cases is the nature—but nature, we say, as form and substance.... Concoction, in fact, is what everything is affected by when its matter—that is, its liquid—is mastered. For this is what is determined by the heat in its nature. For as long as the ratio (*logos*) is in this, the thing has its nature. (*Mete*. 379^{b}18–35)

Natural heat is thus *formative* heat—the thing in nature partly responsible for the coming to be and preservation of things, like human beings, that are complex compounds of matter and form.

Uniform stuffs, as minimally formed, have a low level of such heat. As form is added, so that stuffs come to constitute the structural parts of animals (such as hands and eyes), and these to constitute whole animals of different degrees of complexity, natural heat increases: "the more complete ones are hotter in nature and wetter and not earthy" (*GA* 732ᵇ31–32). Such animals more completely pass on their form to offspring (733ᵃ33–ᵇ2). Since human beings are the most complete or most perfect of the sublunary animals (737ᵇ26–27), they are also hottest and most estimable of them:

> All animals with lungs breathe...Why some have this part, and why those having it need to breathe, is that the more estimable of the animals are hottest. For at the same time their soul must have been made more estimable, since they have a more estimable nature than the cold ones. Hence too... that animal in which the blood in the lung is purest and most plentiful is the most upright, namely, man. The cause due to which he alone has his upper part directed to the upper part of the universe is that he possesses such a part. (*Juv.* 477ᵃ13–23)

Although male and female human beings both have formative heat, its level is not the same in each. This is revealed by the different roles played by their respective spermatic products in reproduction—semen (*gonê*) or seed (*sperma*) in the case of males, menses (*katamênia*) in that of females: "the male provides both the form and the starting-point of movement, while the female provides the body, that is, the matter" (*GA* 729ᵃ9–11).

What semen does to menses to form them into a fetus is likened to what a carpenter does to wood to make it into a piece of furniture:

> Nothing comes away from the carpenter to the matter of the pieces of wood he works on, nor is there any part of the craft of carpentry in what is being produced, but the shape—that is, the form—is produced from the carpenter by means of the movement in the matter, that is, his soul, in which the form is present, and his scientific knowledge move his hands or some other part with a certain sort of movement—distinct when what comes to be from it is distinct, the same when what comes to be from it is the same—and the hands move the instruments, and the instruments move the matter. Similarly, the nature present in the male, in those that emit seed, uses the seed as an instrument and as possessing active movement, just as in craft productions the tools are in movement. For the movement of the craft is in a way in them. (*GA* 730^{b}11–23)

In the way that the movement of the carpenter's hands has its starting-point in the form (or formula) of the product present in his soul, then, the movement in the semen has its starting-point in a form—namely, that of the male progenitor. Hence the very same formal constituents exemplified as capacities in his form are exemplified as movements in his semen, guaranteeing that these movements are (at least to begin with) formally identical to the capacities that transmit them: "when it comes into the uterus it composes and moves the female's residue with just the same movement that it is moving with itself" (*GA* 737ᵃ20–22). Were this not so, their transmission to semen could not result in the transmission of the male's form to the offspring.

What enables the transmission of such movements to seed is, first, that they are present in the male's blood—where, encoded in formative heat, they are responsible for the preservation of his form—and, second, that seed itself is a very concentrated or concocted blood product:

> That blood is the last stage of the nourishment in blooded animals, and its analogue in bloodless ones, has been said previously. And since semen too is a residue of nourishment, that is, from its last stage, it will be either blood, its analogue, or something composed of these. And since each of the parts is produced from blood as it is being concocted and somehow divided into parts, and since the non-concocted seed—although quite different from blood when, having been concocted, it is secreted—that is forced out by too frequent indulgence in sexual intercourse is sometimes still bloodlike when it has come out, it is evident that the seed will be a residue of nourishment, namely, of the blood, the one that

> is finally distributed to the parts. And because of this it has great capacity (and in fact the discharge of the pure and healthy blood is apt to cause weakness) and that offspring should be like their parents is reasonable. For what has gone to the parts is like what is left over. So the seed of the hand, of the face, or of the whole animal is in an undifferentiated way a hand, a face, or a whole animal—that is, as each of the latter is actually, such the seed is potentially. (*GA* 726^{b}1–18)

When the male's formal movements are transmitted by concoction to menses, therefore, they first initiate the formation of the fetal heart. Once the heart is formed, the fetus then grows automatically, drawing its nourishment from its mother through the umbilicus, and in the process transmitting formative movements via the blood to the other developing parts (*GA* 735^{a}12–26).

Menses, however, are also a type of seed—"seed that is not pure, but needs working on" (*GA* 728^{a}26–27). For a female's formative heat is cooler than a male's, and so cannot complete the final stage of forming or concocting menses into pure seed (728^{a}18–21). Nonetheless, a female can concoct her menses (or the spermatic residue in it) to within that last stage of becoming pure seed, so that for each actual movement in seed, there is a corresponding potential movement stemming from the female form (768^{a}11–14). While menses have the potential to move in such a way as to become a fetus, therefore, they cannot do so until they are set moving by semen, since "so far as things formed by nature or by human craft are concerned, the formation of what is potentially is brought about by what is actually" ($734^{a}29$–31). Equally well, of course, without menses to move, no new animal is generated either.

Just which movements will underlie the offspring's form—whether, for example, it will be male or female—depends on the interaction between the movements in the semen and the potential movements in the menses (*GA* $768^{b}5$–12). If a male movement is transmitted successfully to the menses, the offspring will have the corresponding component of the male form. If it fails to be transmitted, it may be wholly resisted, in which case it is replaced by the opposing movement in the menses, or resisted to a lesser degree, with different consequences in each case ($768^{a}7$–9, $768^{b}7$–8).

The resources of the theory

For example, one of the potential movements in a daughter's menses may, as geneticists now put it, *code for* the formation of brown eyes, because her father had brown eyes, and these were transmitted successfully to her mother's menses when the daughter was conceived. Her own son, as a result, has his maternal grandfather's brown eyes, not his own father's blue ones, because the movements that coded for the brown ones successfully resisted (were not "mastered" by) the movements that coded for the blue ones. Since this applies quite generally to all heritable characteristics the explanatory resources of the theory, which anticipate the discovery of recombinant DNA, are immensely rich. Aristotle was a great and pioneering biologist as well as a great philosopher.

The difference between male semen and the seed in female menses, then, is in one way quite small: they both encode more or less the same genetic information, as we would say. But in another way it is quite large: only male semen contains that information as actual movements, making it "the first thing containing a starting-point of generation" (*GA* 724^{b}12–14) (leaving aside possible species in which female seed also contains it). The question is how does the semen encode this information?

Semen, as we now know, is made up of individual sperms, and each viable sperm is in principle capable of fertilizing a female ovum. Aristotle's view is quite different. For him the quantity of semen ejaculated is the fertilizing agent, not its sub-parts, and its viability, to call it that, depends on the level of formative or soul-producing heat in it relative to the quantity of female menses that it must work up:

> In general, then, female and male are set apart from each other in relation to production of

> males and production of females due to the causes just mentioned. Nonetheless there must also be a proportion in their relation to each other. For all things that come to be either in accord with craft or nature exist in virtue of a certain ratio (*logos*). Now the hot, if it too is mastering, dries up the wet things, whereas if it is very deficient it does not compose them, instead it must stand in the mean ratio (*logos*) in relation to what is being handicrafted. If it does not, just as in cooking where too much fire burns the food, while too little does not cook it, and either way the result is that what is being produced fails to be completed, likewise too in the case of the mixing of what comes from the male and what comes from the female there must be a proportion. (*GA* 767^a13–23)

Nonetheless, if the menses is not to be uniformly concocted, but rather differentially so, in the way requisite for stage-wise embryonic development, in which first the fetal heart is formed, then the parts around the head, and so on, the semen too, as Aristotle recognizes, must be "somehow divided into parts" (*GA* 726^b5–6). Nothing is said explicitly about how this division actually takes place. But since semen is foamy, and foam contains bubbles, it is likely that the surrounding membranes of these are what mark the divisions, and encapsulate the formative heat in them:

> The cause of the whiteness of seed is that the semen is foam, and foam is white, and most so that composed of the smallest particles, and small in the way that each bubble is invisible, just as actually happens in the case when water and olive oil are mixed and beaten. (*GA* 736ª13–18)

It seems, then, that we should think of the male semen as somehow divided into bubbles, with different ones embodying the different movements needed to form the different parts of the embryo, and to endow them in turn with the formative heat needed for their growth and preservation. Thus it is that we hear about "the proper heat present in each part" (*GA* 786ª20–21).

While seed, as a concocted blood product, is a very purified type of nourishment, its natural heat, in which its formative movements are encoded, is of a quite special sort:

> Now the capacity of all soul seems to be associated with a body distinct from and more divine than the so-called elements. And as souls differ from each other in esteem and lack of esteem so too this sort of nature differs. For within the seed of everything there is present that which makes the seeds be fertile, the so-called hot. This is not fire or that sort of capacity, but the pneuma enclosed within the seed and within the foamy part—that is, the nature in the pneuma, which is an analogue of the element belonging to the stars. (*GA* 736ᵇ29–737ª1)

Characterized as "connate" (*sumphuton*), because it is not drawn in from outside but produced and maintained inside the body (*PA* 648ᵃ36–649ᵇ8), it is the sort of pneuma that plays a fundamental role in nourishment and reproduction (*GA* 741ᵇ37–742ᵃ16).

The reproductive system

The reproductive system, indeed, is in many ways simply a means of transmitting the form-preserving digestive system (of which blood and the heart are parts) into new matter, thereby initiating the formation of a new self-maintaining creature. That is why both functions are assigned to the *threptikon* or nutritive part of the soul (*DA* 416ᵃ19–20). Aristotle, of course, knew nothing about the central nervous system, or indeed about the circulation of the blood. He could—and did—do autopsies on other species, but not on human beings, which was outlawed.

Although many natural beings (for example, ones we think of as inanimate) do not preserve their form by means of nourishment, or transmit it by means of sexual reproduction, pneuma has a fundamental role to play in their existence, too:

> Democritus, however, omitting to mention the for-the-sake-of-which, reduces to necessity all that nature uses—but though they are such, they are nonetheless

> for the sake of something and in each case for the sake of what is better. So nothing prevents the teeth from being produced and being shed in the way he says, but it is not because of these things, but rather because of the end—although these are causes as movers, as instruments, and as matter, since it is reasonable, indeed, for nature to make most things using pneuma as instrument. For just as some things have many uses where the crafts are concerned—as in blacksmithing are the hammer and the anvil—so does pneuma in those composed by nature. (*GA* 789^{b}2–12)

Yet despite its manifest importance, no focused discussion of pneuma occurs in Aristotle's extant works. This makes it difficult to determine his views with confidence. But by piecing together what he does say, a reasonably clear picture emerges.

From its role in embryology alone, for example, we can see that pneuma transmits movement by being itself in movement. The role accorded to it in animal movement confirms this fact:

> [Pneuma] is evidently well disposed by nature to impart movement and supply strength. At all events, the functions of movement are pushing and pulling, so that its instrument must be capable of increasing in size and contracting. And this is just the nature of pneuma, since it increases in size and contracts unforcedly, and is able to pull and push for the same reason. (*MA* 703^{a}18–23)

Moreover, because the movements it imparts are formative, they must be complex and various—able to code for all an animal's parts. Since movements are "either in a circle or in a straight line or in a combination of the two" (*Ph.* 261^{b}28–29), all the complex movements pneuma can produce must be some such combination. What makes this possible is that by actively expanding and contracting inside bubbles, and so pushing and pulling, it can cause not just rectilinear but also circular movements: "Spinning in a circle is a compound of pushing and pulling, since what causes something to spin must be pushing one part of it and pulling another, for it draws one part away from itself and another part toward itself" (244^{a}2–4). Hence all movements—rectilinear, circular, or a combination of the two—can be caused by pneuma in combination with earth, water, and the other elements. (*DA* 433^{b}25–26)

Initially pneuma is assigned a role in the transmission of form to non-controversially animate beings. But its role gets expanded to explain other phenomena:

> It is not insofar as something is water or insofar as it is air that it is visible, but because there is a certain nature in it that is the same in both of them and in the [eternal] body above. (*DA* 418^{b}7–9)

Then, because pneuma is involved in soul-transmission, soul is to some extent itself attributed to anything in which pneuma is present: "Animals and plants come to be on earth and in liquid because in earth there is water present and in water pneuma, and in all pneuma there is soul-involving heat, so that in a certain way all things are full of soul" (*GA* $762^{a}18$–21). When "the capacity of all soul" is associated with the nature in the pneuma that is an analogue of the element belonging to the stars, then, the point of analogy is that the nature in question is both transparent and—when combined with other elements, whose movements are rectilinear—an appropriate transmitter of soul, form, and life. For the element that belongs to the stars, which is *ether* (*aithêr*) or primary body (*sôma prôton*), is a body "different from and additional to the elemental ones met with here, more divine than, and prior to, all of them" (*Cael.* $269^{a}30$–32), and is both transparent and in eternal circular movement ($270^{a}12$–$^{b}25$). Hence pneuma is a "body more divine than the so-called elements," because it is an analogue of ether, which is in fact more divine than they.

Focusing now on pneuma, let us see how best to understand it. One thing we know is that "it increases in size and contracts unforcedly, and is able to pull and push for the same reason" (*MA* $703^{a}21$–22), but another is that it is "hot air" (*GA* $736^{a}1$)—air that includes formative heat. Putting the two together we have air increasing in size and contracting due to heat, presumably inside bubbles of the relevant sort.

Pneuma is not a new element

Pneuma is not a new element, then, but rather a construction from old ones introduced to explain the existence in the sublunary world of the circular movements crucial for the transmission and preservation of forms, and so for the coming to be and passing away of the matter-form compounds whose forms they are.

But pneuma is equally central to the explanation of animal movement, perception, and thought:

> The movement of animals is like that of automata, which are set moving when a small movement occurs: the strings are released and the pegs strike against one another. . . . For animals have instrumental parts that are of the same sort as these, namely, sinews and bones; when these are relaxed or loosened movement occurs. . . . In an animal, however, [unlike in an automaton] the same part is capable of becoming both larger and smaller and to change its shape, as the parts increase in size because of heat, contract again because of cold, and undergo alteration. Alteration, however, is caused by appearances, perceptions, and intelligible objects. For perceptions are an immediate sort of alteration,

and appearances and intelligible objects have the capacity of the things themselves [that gave rise to them]. For in a way the intelligible form of the pleasant or painful is like the thing itself. That is why we shudder and are frightened because of understanding on its own. All these are affections and alterations; and when things in the body are altered, some become larger and some smaller. And it is not hard to see that a small change occurring in a starting-point produces great and numerous changes at a distance from it—just as by shifting the rudder a hair's breadth you get a large shift at the prow. Besides, when under the influence of heat or cold or some other similar affection, an alteration is produced in the region of the heart, even in an imperceptibly small part of it, it produces a large difference in the body—blushing, for example, or turning white, as well as shuddering, trembling, and their opposites. (*MA* 701^b1–32)

Form of every variety, one might almost say, just is a sort of movement.

The Inheritance of Understanding

To this account of the transmission of form and soul from parents to offspring, the inheritance of a part of our soul called *nous* (understanding) is an intriguing exception, since it alone among the human soul's activities has no correlate in the (sublunary) body: "bodily activity is in no way associated with its activity" (*GA* 736^{b}28–29). The puzzle immediately arises of how what is without such a correlate can develop in a fetus as a result of movements in the pneuma contained in male seed:

> It is necessary to determine whether what is being composed in the female receives something, or not, from what has entered her, but also, concerning the soul in virtue of which an animal is so called (and it is an animal in virtue of the perceptual part of the soul), whether it is present within the seed and the fetus or not, and where it comes from [if it is]. For one could not regard the fetus as soulless, as in every way lacking in life. For both the seeds and the embryos of animals are no less alive than plants, and are fertile up to a certain point. That they have nutritive soul, then, is evident (and why they must acquire this first is evident from the determinations about the soul made elsewhere), but as they proceed they also have perceptual soul in virtue of which they are animals. For they do not at the same time become animal and human, or animal and horse, and likewise in the case of the other animals. For the last thing to come to be is the end, and the end of the coming to be of each thing is what is special to it. That is why where understanding

> is concerned, when, how, and from where it is acquired by those that participate in this starting-point, involves a very great puzzle, and we must try hard to get a grasp on [these things] in accord with our capacity and to the extent possible. (*GA* 736ᵃ27–ᵇ8)

The reason it is such a puzzle is that the various psychological functions can be present as capacities or potentials in seed or fetus in only a certain number of ways:

> For **[1]** either they must all be produced [in the menses or matter] without existing beforehand, or they must all preexist, or some must, but not others; and **[2]** they must be produced in the matter either without having entered in the male's seed, or having come from there; and **[3]** in the male they must either all be produced [in the seed] from outside it, or none from outside, or some but not others. Now then that it is impossible for all to be present beforehand is evident from the following. For **[4]** it is clear that it is impossible for all starting-points whose activity is bodily to be present without body (for example, walking without feet). So **[5]** they cannot enter [the seed] from outside. For they can neither enter by themselves, being inseparable [from matter], nor enter in a body. For the seed is a residue produced by a change in the nutriment. **[6]** It remains, then,

> that the understanding alone enters additionally from outside and alone is divine. For bodily activity is in no way associated with its activity. (*GA* 736b15–29)

Here **[1]** concerns the menses and what it contributes to the fetus; **[2]** concerns the seed and what it contributes; and **[3]** concerns the male progenitor and what he contributes to the seed. And the line of descent, as we know, is from formative movements in the pneuma contained in the male progenitor's blood to his seed, from seed to menses, and so to fetus. **[4]** restricts our attention to starting-points of psychological functions whose active varieties are bodily, in that they require bodily organs, as walking requires feet and seeing requires eyes. **[5]** tells us the two conditions under which these could enter something "from the outside." This signal, as **[3]** makes clear, that the something they enter is the male seed. **[5]** then shows that the starting-points cannot meet either of the conditions: they cannot enter by themselves, apart from body, because they are inseparable from it; they cannot enter as a body, because seed does not contain parts, such as hands or eyes. On the other hand, **[6]** because bodily activity is in no way associated with the activity of understanding, understanding does enter the male seed from outside. That is the picture.

Just how understanding manages to enter the seed from outside is left unexplained, and we may leave it so for a moment. All that we are told is that in embryogenesis it is transmitted along with the seed yet separate from it:

> As for the body of the semen, in which comes away part of the seed of the soul-involving starting-point, part of which is separable from the body in all the ones in which a divine something is enclosed (and what is called the understanding is of this sort) and part inseparable—this body of the semen dissolves and evaporates, having a liquid and watery nature. (*GA* 737ᵃ7–12)

Nonetheless, as a result of being transmitted in this way, the understanding "seems to be born in us as a sort of substance, and not to pass away" (*DA* 408ᵇ18–25) and to be "presumably something more divine" (408ᵇ29). Moreover, it is "in substance an activity," and so is not "sometimes understanding and at other times not," but rather of all the elements in the human soul "it alone is immortal and eternal" (430ᵃ18–23). These characteristics make it reasonable to suppose that understanding is transmitted along with the male seed as movements in *ether* that code for it. The following description of ether makes the supposition all but certain:

> It is equally reasonable to suppose about this body [= ether] that it is incapable of coming to be and passing away, incapable of increase and decrease,

and incapable of alteration, because everything that comes to be comes to be from its contrary and from an underlying subject, and passes away similarly, namely, from an underlying subject, because of a contrary, and to a contrary, as was said in our first accounts [in *Ph.* I 7–9]. Also, contrary spatial movements are of contraries. If, then, this body can have no contrary, because there cannot in fact be a movement contrary to spatial movement in a circle, nature seems to have correctly removed from among the contraries the body that was going to be incapable of coming to be and passing away. For coming to be and passing away belong in the realm of contraries. But then too everything that increases, increases because of something of the same genus being added to it and dissolving into its matter. But there is none from which this body has come to be. But if it is not capable of either increase or decrease, the same thinking leads us to suppose that it is not capable of alteration either. For alteration is movement with respect to quality, and qualitative states and dispositions—for example, health and disease—do not come about without change with respect to the affections. But all natural [sublunary] bodies that change with respect to an affection we see are subject both to increase and decrease—for example, the bodies of animals and plants and their parts, and also those of the elements. So if indeed the body in circular

> movement does not admit of either increase or decrease, it is reasonable for it to be unalterable as well. (*Cael.* 270a12–35)

If understanding were coded for by anything other than the circular movements in ether, indeed, it seems that it could not itself be immortal, eternal, or ever active.

We may now return to the question of how understanding manages to enter the seed from outside. Aristotle, as I said, does not specifically address this question. But it is possible to take a few speculative steps toward an answer, by beginning with a text from *De Mundo*, a work which, though attributed to Aristotle, is almost certainly not by him, and by following out a path to which it leads:

> There is indeed an ancient account, native to all human beings, that the composition of all things derives from a god and is due to a god, and that no nature whatsoever is intrinsically self-sufficient if deprived of the preservation deriving from this…, [which is] an account fitting for the divine capacity, but not for its substance [or essence]. For the god is really the preserver of all things and the begetter (*genetôr*) of everything in this cosmos, in whatever way it is brought to completion, without indeed taking upon himself the toil of an animal that works and endures hardship for itself, but making use of an untiring capacity, by means of

> which he prevails even over things that seem to be a long way off. (*Mu.* 397b13–24)

Let us suppose that even if these are not Aristotle's words, they at least present a genuine strain in his thought, when they make a god stand to the universe in the way that a human male generator stands to a human female, namely, by supplying an immaterial starting-point of formative movements to what cannot autonomously move itself. Think now of the role of the seasons, as determined by the sun's relationship to the earth, and their role in determining the fertility and infertility, growth and withering away, of plants and animals—a role that is being acknowledged in this text:

> The cause of a human is both his elements, fire and earth as matter and the special form [as form], and furthermore some other external thing, such as the father, and beyond these *the sun and its movement in an inclined circle*. (*Met.* 1071a13–16)

Now think of the god we are discussing as responsible (in a way we shall explore in Chapter 5) for the sun's movements, and of their effects on the ether in the male seed, whose movements code for understanding. While the human male is the starting-point of the movements that transmit other capacities of soul to the female menses, so that these are internal to it, god alone is the starting-point for those responsible for the transmission of understanding.

Ether

Ether, to be sure, is a bit hard to get a handle on, since it seems, for one thing, to be a sort of perpetual motion machine—something that by its very essence cannot be inactive or run out of steam. At the same time, though, it is fairly clearly something material. Hence the understanding, which is coded for by its movements, while it can come apart from earth, water, air, and fire, cannot ever become wholly disembodied. Its entry into the male seed in embryogenesis, then, is not a case of a ghost entering a machine, but—to continue the metaphor—of one sort of machine entering another. This lessens the mystery that understanding seemed to present us with even if it does not dispel it altogether.

We are likely to—and perhaps should—see these views about *nous* as relatives of religious doctrines about the immortality of the human soul. They are especially close to specifically Roman Catholic doctrines, which see human reason (the analogue of *nous*) as implanted by God in a developing embryo, whose other psychological capacities (perception, memory, and so on) may be explained, in an essentially Darwinian way, as the results of evolutionary forces.

Chapter 3

Soul, Perception, and Understanding

The fact that soul is transmitted in the way we have just been exploring has consequences for what an Aristotelian soul is. Female menses is a complex structure of potential movements. As such, it is lifeless and soulless—unmoving. When the male semen, with its bubbles of pneuma, enters it and causes ongoing movements within it, the resulting embryo acquires nutritive soul (*GA* 736ᵃ35–36).

As a result, the seed has the capacity to take in nourishment and grow, when it is in a functioning female uterus where menses are available to nourish it. And because it does Aristotle can define soul generally—whether nutritive (as in plants) or perceptive (as in animals) or rational (as in human beings)—as "the first actualization (*entelecheia*) of a natural body that has life potentially" (*DA* 412^a27–28) or, more expansively, as "the first actualization of a natural instrumental body" (412^b5–6).

For a first capacity or potential is like the capacity someone has to learn Greek. When that capacity is actualized through the acquisition of the ability to speak Greek, that is its *first-stage* actuality—the first stage in the actualization of the capacity. The acquired capacity he now has to exercise his acquired ability in actively speaking Greek is a second-stage capacity or potential—a second stage in the development of the original first-stage capacity. Actualizing that second capacity in actively speaking, in turn, is a *second-stage* actuality (417^a21–29) or activity (*energeia*) (*Met.* 1043^a35–36). Thus in a mature animal the capacity for nourishment and growth is always possessed as a *first-stage* actuality as long as the animal is alive. It is only in the seed from which it develops that nutritive soul is present as a *first-stage* capacity or potential: "It is not what has lost its soul that is potentially such as to live, but what has it. The seed and the fruit are potentially bodies of this sort" (*DA* 412^b26–27).

Pneuma, as we saw, when properly encapsulated in the bubbles in the semen is a sort of vitalizing factor, the one that brings life and soul *into the right sort of body*, equipping it with the starting-points of the various life or soul functions. In the case of a seed, the right sort of body is a natural one with parts that can serve as instruments of nourishment and growth. In the case of a capacity, such as the capacity to walk, whose actualization requires feet as instruments, the natural instrumental body in which they can be present must obviously be of a different sort from seed. Similarly, to have sight as a first actualization, a body needs to have functional eyes. And what makes an eye functional, what makes it a living eye, is that it is appropriately animated or ensouled, appropriately alive. For that to be possible, however, the eye must be part of the living body of an autonomously functioning whole animal—one in whose blood formative movements reach all the various functional parts.

The definition of soul

That is why soul can also be defined as the "form of a natural body that has life potentially" (*DA* 412ª19–21). If the life in question is simply vegetative life, the requisite type of body may be that of a seed, and its form, once it is planted and begins to grow, may be the structure of informing movements that code for nourishment and growth. If the life is that of perception, the requisite body must contain a structure of such movements that is correspondingly more complex.

It is worth noticing how far away such a conception of the soul (the account of *nous* aside) is from more familiar dualistic conceptions of the sort found, for example, in Descartes, or in religious conceptions of the soul that restrict its possession to human beings. So-called functionalist theories of the mind (as the soul's secular analogue), which many philosophers now embrace, are often traced back to Aristotle.

Characteristic of animal souls is the possession of two capacities, which must occur together (*DA* 413^b23–24), one "to judge things and the other to cause movement with respect to place" (432^a15–17). The capacity for judgment is due, first, to the possession of a "perceptual part" (*aisthêtikon*) (432^a30), responsible for perception proper and various other functions, such as imagination. In human beings, this part consists of the *primary perceptual part,* located in the heart, as well as the various special perceptual capacities—sight, smell, hearing, taste, touch—and the common perceptual capacity. The part responsible for movement is the desiring part (*orektikon*). It consists of desires of various sorts, which cause movement or action by being modes of receptivity or responsiveness to aspects of reality judged as pleasant or painful or, in some other way, good or bad, end-furthering or end-frustrating (431^b8–10). Finally, the human soul also contains a rational part, comprising the scientific part (*epistêmonikon*) and the calculative (*logistikon*) or deliberative (*bouleutikon*) one (*NE*

1139^a5–15), as well, of course, as the understanding (*nous*), which, since it is responsible for knowledge of scientific and deliberative starting-points, or first principles (1141^a7–8), is involved in both of them. We shall see more about these later on in the chapter.

Perception

In blooded animals, the perceptual system is part of (or piggybacks on) the digestive system, the perceptual capacities (or senses) being set on channels connected to small blood vessels around the brain, which are connected to the heart by larger vessels in the neck. The heart, as a result, not the brain, is the locus of the "primary perceptual part" (*Somn.* 454^a22–24). Where there is perception, however, there is "also both pleasure and pain, and where these, of necessity appetite too" (*DA* 413^b23–24). Hence the heart is also the locus of pleasure and pain (*PA* 666^a11–13), and of the animal movement to which appetite gives rise (647^a24–31).

Perception proper encompasses the special perceptual capacities (sight, smell, hearing, taste, and touch), whose primary objects are *special perceptibles*, such as colors, odors, sounds, and so on, which only a single perceptual capacity can detect. In addition, the perceptual part includes the common perceptual capacity (*DA* 431^b5). It is responsible for the simultaneous perception of two or more special perceptibles in a single act, the perception of two or more special perceptibles as distinct, the control of waking up the special perceptual capacities or letting them sleep (*Somn.* 455ᵃ12–26), the awareness of the activity or inactivity of the various special perceptual capacities (*DA* 425ᵇ12–25), and perhaps also the perception of *common perceptibles*, which are features accessible to more than one perceptual capacity, such as change, rest, shape, size, number, unity, and perhaps others (425ᵃ14–20). The sphere of perception, therefore, is that of particulars, which are perceptible because they possess attributes that are special or common perceptibles (*NE* 1109ᵇ22–23).

Aristotle's account of perception

Aristotle's account of perception, as indeed of thought and understanding, is dominated by the idea of the transmission of form through imprinting—of something like wax taking on something like the impression of a seal or signet ring: "We should take it as a general truth about all perception that a perceptual capacity is what can receive perceptible forms without their matter, just as wax receives the imprint of the ring without the iron or gold" (*DA* 424ᵃ17–20). (Notice the similarity to the account of the transmission of soul in animal reproduction.) Since sight is "perception par excellence" (429ᵃ2–3), we shall focus on it.

As with any psychological capacity, sight must be explained in terms of its characteristic activity (seeing), and so of the special perceptible object (color), which alone actualizes it (*DA* 415ᵃ14–22). What is directly affected by color is the eye, the organ or instrument of sight, whose form is seeing and whose matter is eye-jelly (*korê*): "seeing . . . is the eye's substance or essence, that which corresponds to its account," and an eye is "the eye-jelly plus sight, [just as] an animal is soul plus body" (412ᵇ18–413ᵃ3). The effect color has on the eye-jelly is determined by its nature, which is determined by its relation to light, whose own nature is determined, in turn, by its relation to transparency:

> For what is visible is color, and it is what is on [the surface of] what is intrinsically visible—intrinsically visible not in account, but because it has within itself the cause of its being visible. For every color is capable of causing movement in what is actually transparent, and this is its nature. That is why it is not visible without light, but rather the color of each thing is always seen in light. Which is why we must first say what light is. There is, then, something transparent. And by transparent I mean what is indeed visible, although not intrinsically visible, simply speaking, but rather visible because of the color of something else. Air, water, and many solid bodies are of this sort. For it is not insofar

> as something is water or insofar as it is air that it is visible, but because there is a certain nature in it that is the same in both of them and in the [eternal] body above. And light is the activity of this, of the transparent insofar as it is transparent. But whatever this is present in, so potentially is darkness. For light is a sort of color of the transparent, when it is made actually transparent by fire or something of that sort, such as the body above. (*DA* 418^{a}29–^{b}13)

The certain nature referred to, which is present in all transparent things, is pneuma, as we saw, which is also present "in all other bodies to a greater or lesser degree" (*Sens.* 439^{a}24–25). That is why opaque objects can be colored. For color just is the surface envelope that such pneuma acquires by being in a bounded body: "The very same thing that is dark or light when in an indefinite or unbounded transparent mass, then, is black or white when it is the limit of a bounded one" (439^{b}14–18). Hence the surface of an object is white just in case the pneuma in it is illuminated (light) and is black when the pneuma is not-illuminated (dark), either because no light is present or because other sublunary matter occludes it, since the "same nature is sometimes darkness and sometimes light" (*DA* 418^{b}31–419^{a}1).

With white and black defined in terms of light and dark, other colors are defined in terms of them:

> It is possible that the white and the black should be so juxtaposed that each is invisible because it is very

small, but that what is composed of both is visible. This can appear neither as white nor as black. But since it must have some color, and cannot have either of these, it must be some kind of mixture, that is, some other kind of color. Such, then, is a possible way of conceiving of the existence of a plurality of colors besides white and black, but which are a plurality because of the ratio [of white to black that constitutes them]; for they [white and black] may be juxtaposed in the ratio 3:2 or 3:4, or in ratios expressible by other numbers, or they may be in no numerically expressible ratio, but in some incommensurable relation of excess or deficiency. (*Sens.* 439^{b}19–30)

For the surface of an object to be colored, therefore, is just for the transparent material within it to be dark (unactualized) or light (actualized) in the appropriate way. While the form of a color is some pattern of black and white, its matter is this dark or light transparent material. (Think again of how formative movements are encapsulated in bubbles in male seed.)

"This is what the being [or essence] is for color, namely, to be capable of causing movement in what is actively transparent… The color causes the transparent—for example, the air—to move, and due to this, when the transparent is continuous, the perceptual organ is moved" (*DA* 419^{a}9–15). In transparent eye-jelly, this movement results in its taking on the visible form of the color without its matter. Thus the eye-jelly takes on a pattern of black and white similar to the one present in the colored surface that is being seen, but without the corresponding dark and light material that is in the body itself.

The reason eye-jelly must be transparent, then, is that it must be able to take on patterns of dark and light in order for the eye to judge colors. For if eye-jelly is to be able to take on any pattern of dark and light that corresponds to a color, it must be in a *mean* or *intermediate* condition between dark and light. And this is the condition transparent material is in, since it is light when illuminated and dark otherwise:

> A perceptual capacity [is] a sort of mean between the pairs of contraries in the perceptible objects. And that is why it judges the perceptible objects. For the mean is capable of judging, since in relation to each extreme it becomes the other. And just as what is to perceive white and black must be neither of them actively, although both potentially (and similarly too in the case of the other perceptual capacities), so in the case of touch it must be neither hot nor cold. (*DA* 424ᵃ5–10)

By taking on a pattern of dark and light, the eye-jelly becomes in "a way colored" itself (*DA* 425ᵇ22–23). Moreover, it can remain in this condition even when color is no longer being seen: "Each perceptual organ is receptive of the perceptible object without its matter. That is why perceptions and appearances remain in the perceptual organs even when the perceptible objects are gone" (425ᵇ23–25).

Perceptual Error

On this account of how perception operates, it might seem that—in the case of special perceptibles, at least—it cannot make errors. And we do find Aristotle claiming this:

> By a special object I mean whatever cannot be perceived by another perceptual capacity, and about which we cannot be deceived—for example, sight is of color, hearing of sound, taste of flavor, whereas touch has several different ones. At any rate, a given perceptual capacity judges about these, and does not make errors about whether there is color or whether there is sound, but rather about what the colored thing is or where it is, or what the thing making the sound is or where it is. (*DA* 418ᵃ11–16).

But these confident claims presuppose that the perceptual capacities are functioning properly in conditions that do not impede their achieving their end (*NE* 1153ᵃ15). For people "do not perceive what is presented to their eyes, if they happen to be deep in thought, or afraid, or hearing a lot of noise" (*Sens.* 447ᵃ15–17) and cannot perceive accurately what is not presented at the right distance (449ᵃ21–24) or in the right way: "each thing is more readily perceptible when presented simply by itself than when mixed with others—for example, pure rather than unmixed wine, or honey, or a color, or a single note rather than one in a chord—because they tend to obscure one another" (447ᵃ17–20).

Yet even when conditions of these sorts are met, room for error still remains. For "perceptions persist after the external perceptible object has gone" (*Insomn.* 460ᵇ2–4), as we saw, with the result that things appear to us as they do "when the perceptible object produces the movement [in the perceptual capacity], but also when the perceptual capacity is moved by itself, provided it is moved in a similar way to the one in which the object falling under the perceptual capacity moves it" (460ᵇ22–25). When, for example, we "have looked for a long time at a single color—such as white or green—any object to which we shift our gaze appears to be of that very color" (459ᵇ11–13). So we can be deceived even about whether the color is there in front of our eyes. It is presumably with such cases in mind that Aristotle modifies his bold claims about inerrancy. Perception of the special perceptibles is "true or has the least possible degree of falsity" (*DA* 428ᵇ18–19), at any rate, "as long as the perception is present" (428ᵇ27–28), that is to say, while the perceptible object continues to affect the perceptual capacity in the right way.

What we typically perceive, however, is not one isolated special perceptible, but an array of many different ones. And this raises a problem that Aristotle discusses in some detail. A single (act of) perception must have a single object at a single unified time, since that is just what makes it *one perception*. Thus it is not possible to have "one perception of two things at the same time," since the perception "of one thing is itself one thing, and what is one thing occurs at the same time as itself" (*Sens.* 447b9–11). It seems to follow that we cannot see and taste the same thing simultaneously, and so cannot perceive that bile is both "bitter and yellow" (*DA* 425b1–2). Nonetheless, access to complexes of special perceptibles *is* directly perceptual (*Sens.* 449a5–20). When we see the yellow of honey, for example, while simultaneously tasting its sweetness, we do so by means of one part of the soul—the perceptual part. Because yellow and sweetness differ in genus (one a color, the other a taste), the account we give of this part as perceiving yellow will refer to one genus of it (sight), while the account we give of it as perceiving sweetness will refer to a different one (taste). If, instead, the perception were of a yellow and black wasp, the accounts of the perceptual part as seeing yellow and as seeing black would refer to different species (yellow, black) of the same genus (color).

The different perceptual capacities are not numerically distinct parts of the perceptual part, then, but different aspects of its functioning, just as the different at- tributes of a single substance (the wasp, the honey) are different aspects of it—different in being or essence, or in the account we give of them, but not separate from it. Hence when we perceive sweet and yellow honey or a black and yellow wasp, we do not infer or construct the perceived object from the simple special perceptibles involved, but perceive it directly as one single thing by using two or more distinct perceptual capacities simultaneously (*DA* 425ᵃ22–24). Although Aristotle does not say that such perception cannot make errors, there is no reason to think that it is any more prone to them than the perception of simple special perceptibles: a wasp's color is not a confusion of black and yellow, after all, but a clear pattern of black and yellow stripes. Consequently, perception's degree of error should be the same in both cases.

As the objects to which "the substance or essence of each perceptual capacity is naturally related," special perceptibles are the most basic objects of perception—those on which the perception of other things depends (*DA* 418ᵃ24–25). They are not the only objects that are intrinsically perceptible, however, since common perceptibles, such as shape, that are accessible to more than one perceptual capacity are also such (418ᵃ8–11). Complexes of special and common perceptibles—of the sort presented by substantial matter-form particulars like ourselves—are thus directly perceptible: no inference is required. It is universal forms of these, however, that are imprinted on the perceptual capacities (as patterns of black and white are on the eye-jelly), not the particular matter-form compounds whose forms they are: "we perceive particulars, but perception is of universals—for example, of man and not of Callias the man" (*APo.* 100ᵃ16–ᵇ1). These forms are presented to the perceptual capacity as wholes, because the task of articulating them—of defining them in terms of their constituents and explanatory starting-points—belongs to science, not perception:

> The things that are in the first instance clear and perspicuous to us are rather confused. It is only later, through a division of these, that we come to know their elements and starting-points. That is why we must proceed from the universals to the particulars. For it is the whole that is more knowable by perception, and the universal is a sort of whole. For the universal embraces many things as parts. The same thing happens in a way with names in relation to their account. For a name like "circle" signifies a sort of whole in an undivided way, whereas the definition divides it into its particular [elements]. And children at first suppose all men to be their fathers and all women their mothers, only later coming to divide up each of them. (*Ph.* 184ᵃ21–ᵇ14)

When we perceive Callias, the various special and common perceptibles constituting his perceptible form are imprinted on the various perceptual capacities (or correlative organs) constituting our perceptible part, so that the structure of the one—a single subject possessed of various universal attributes—is mirrored in the structure of the other.

In his discussion of place or location (*topos*), Aristotle claims that place "would not be a subject of inquiry if movement with respect to place did not exist" (*Ph.* 211^{a}12–13). For we become aware of places by perceiving the replacement of one thing by another:

> That place exists seems to be clear from replacement. For where there is now water, there, when the water has gone out as from a vessel, air is in turn present. Then some other bodies occupy this same place. (*Ph.* 208^{b}1–4)

Place, however, seems to be a common perceptible, since movement, which is a common perceptible, is change with respect to it.

In the case of place, the change or movement at issue is change in the object of perception. It is also the sort at issue in the case of continuity—anyway, of the sort possessed by the complexes of special and common perceptibles that constitute the perceptible forms of substantial matter-form compounds (*Met.* 1052^{a}22–26).

Perceptible forms

Here the perceptual analogue of the substance's own cohesiveness and continuity of movement is the continuous multi-sense perception of it that constitutes our perceptual tracking of it through space and time. For the temporal unity of a single (act of) perception need not be that of a temporal point but may be an extended period whose unity is (in part) determined by—or off-loaded onto—that of its object: "things that are indivisible, though, not with respect to quantity, but in form, a person understands in an indivisible time and with an indivisible part of the soul" (*DA* 430^{a}14–15). Perceptible forms, we may infer, are not static gestalts, or fixed arrays of special and common perceptibles, but dynamic unities, more akin to films than photographs—analogues, in fact, of the forms transmitted in embryogenesis.

When we perceive white, our perception is quite reliable, but when we perceive that the white thing "is this, or something else, [perception] can be false" (*DA* 428^{b}21–22). In these cases, the "this, or something else" is a *coincidental perceptible*, such as the son of Cleon, whom we perceive "not because he is the son of Cleon, but because he is white, and this the son of Cleon happens to be" (425^{a}25–27). It is a person's perception of coincidental perceptibles that fear or some other appetite or feeling can distort, so that he "seems, even from a very slight resemblance, to see his enemy" (*Insomn.* 460ᵇ6–7), and so is deceived.

What makes deception of this sort possible is, first, that imagination-based appearances can have the very same content as the perceptions that cause them, and, second, that the perceptual part of the soul can operate in isolation from the rational part:

> Imagination [is] a movement that comes about as a result of the activity of perception... And because its objects persist and are similar to perceptions, animals do many things in accord with them, some because they lack understanding (for example, beasts) and others because their understanding is sometimes obscured by feeling, disease, or sleep (for example, human beings). (*DA* 429ᵃ1–8)

The resulting deception is, therefore, of two types, one occurring when the perceptible object is present to the perceptual capacities, the other when it is absent (*DA* 428ᵇ27–29). When the perceptible object is a special perceptible, no deception of the first type is possible: only an appearance of *white* sufficiently resembles a perception of white to lead the perceptual part to take it for such an appearance. Hence deception is possible only about the presence of the object to sight, not about its identity. In the case of coincidental perceptibles and common perceptibles, on the other hand, both types of deception are possible, though there are important differences between them.

Even when a white thing that is being perceived is the son of Cleon, neither the resulting perception nor the longer-lasting appearance may be precise enough to distinguish him from many other people. Nonetheless, when the perception or appearance *is* sufficiently detailed and precise it can, like an accurate portrait, provide a reliable basis for identification—although not, of course, when the object is far away (*DA* 428^{b}29). In the case of common perceptibles, by contrast, even a very detailed and precise perception or appearance will not provide a reliable basis for judging between sizes, shapes, numbers, and speeds, if they differ from one another in ways the perceptual capacities alone, in isolation from the rational part, cannot detect. The point goes back to Plato:

> The same object, viewed from nearby, does not appear the same size, I presume, as when viewed from a distance… And the same things appear bent and straight when seen in water or out of it, or concave and convex because sight is misled by colors, and every other similar sort of confusion is clearly present in our soul… And haven't measuring, counting, and weighing proved to be most welcome assistants in these cases, ensuring that what appears bigger or smaller or more numerous or heavier does not rule within us, but rather what has calculated or measured or even weighed?… And that is the task of the soul's rational constituent?… [And it] believes in accord with the measurements. (*Republic* 602d–603e)

Aristotle's thought is similar. Perception makes errors where common perceptibles are concerned when operating in isolation from the rational part of the soul, and the measuring instruments, calculating devices, and various sorts of scientific theories that cannot exist without it.

In human beings and in other animals, the fact that perception gives rise to imagination and appearances leads to various sorts of deception and error. That is the downside, as it were, of having an imagination. But there is also a substantial upside. Appearances are crucial to memory, since they make up its contents (*Mem.* 451^{a}14–16); memory is crucial to induction and the development of scientific knowledge (topics explored in Chapter 5). They are also crucial to thought of all sorts, including understanding: "appearances serve as perceptions to the soul that involves thought," since when "someone understands, he must simultaneously understand an appearance" (*DA* 431^{a}14–16). Hence while perception's inerrancy is limited, its *influence* extends to the very highest reaches of knowledge (*APr.* 46^{a}17–22). Once scientific knowledge has been acquired, moreover, its application in particular cases re-involves perception, since we have to perceive that this particular thing is, for example, a human being in order to know what the science of human beings has to say about it. The form the eye-jelly takes on in any sort of perception is a universal, but what is perceived, as we saw, is the particular that has the form (*Met.* 1087^{a}19–21).

Thus, in contrast to scientific knowledge, which is knowledge of universals, perception is the capacity of the soul, which, by judging particulars, gives us cognitive access to them and thereby to the universals we reach by induction from them (*APo.* 81^{a}38–^{b}6).

Desire

The desiring part of the soul comprises appetite (*epithumia*), spirit (*thumos*), and wish (*boulêsis*) (*EE* 1223^{a}26–27). “Appetite is concerned with what is pleasant and what is painful” (*NE* 1111^{b}16–17), and is relatively straightforward. It moves us to pursue the pleasant and avoid the painful.

Spirit is more complicated. Aristotle often uses the terms *thumos* and *orgê* (“anger”) interchangeably (*Rh.* 1369^{a}7, ^{b}11), and very often uses *thumos* in contexts where its aggressive side is highlighted (*NE* 1116^{b}15–1117^{a}9). In other places, however, he says only that anger is “in” the spirited part of the soul (*Top.* 113^{a}36–^{b}1), alongside other feelings, such as fear and hatred (126^{a}8–9). And in one passage he identifies spirit as the source not just of “negative” feelings but also of love and friendship: “spirit is what produces friendliness, since it is the capacity of the soul by which we love” (*Pol.* 1327^{b}40–1328^{a}1). Presumably, then, we should think of spirit as passionate—as “hot and hasty” (*NE* 1149^{a}30)—rather than as always aggressive.

Wish is more complex still. On what we might call the *official view* wish seems to be the quintessential thought-involving desire (*NE* 1139ᵇ5). For wish is "always found in the rationally calculative part" of the soul (*Top.* 126ᵃ13), so that "when something is moved in accord with rational calculation, it is moved in accord with wish" (*DA* 433ᵃ23–25). For "wish is a desire for the good (for no one wishes for something except what he thinks good)" (*Rh.* 1369ᵃ2–4), and to figure out what our good is in particular circumstances requires thought and deliberation. Should I have the salad or the Big Mac, join the Resistance or take care of my sick mother?

In the *Politics*, however, Aristotle seems to deviate from the official view: "spirit and wish, and furthermore appetite, are present in children straight from birth, whereas rational calculation and understanding naturally arise as they grow" (1334ᵇ22–25). But the explanation for the deviation is not far to seek. For when Aristotle discusses wish in the process of trying to explain deliberate choice (*prohairesis*), he writes:

> [Deliberate choice] is not wish either, although it appears to be a close relative of it. For there is no deliberate choice of impossible things, and if someone were to say he was deliberately choosing them, he would seem silly. But there is wish for impossible things—for example, immortality. There is also wish concerning the sorts of things

> that could never come about through ourselves—for example, that a certain actor or athlete should win a victory prize. No one deliberately chooses things like that, but things he thinks can come about through him. Further, wish is more for the end, whereas deliberate choice is of the things that further the end. (*NE* 1111ᵇ19–27)

Understood in this way, there seems to be nothing especially rational about wish, which makes it easy to see why children are said to have it. This suggests that *boulêsis* is being used in two different ways—the first technical, the second loose and popular.

There is a way, however, to reconcile the two uses. And this lies in the very definition of wish itself as a desire that is "unconditionally and in truth… [for] the good" but in each individual for "the apparent good" (*NE* 1113ᵃ23–24). So what we ought to say is that wish, as a desire for the apparent good, is present in children straight from birth, but that with the proper habituation and training what appears good them can be the real good, with the result that wish becomes properly responsive to the deliberation that best furthers that good, by having its starting-point and cause in that deliberation.

Besides its distinctive location in the rationally calculative part of the soul and its distinctive relation to calculation and deliberation, then, wish is also distinctive in being the sort of desire we have for happiness or the good, or what appears to us as such.

We wish for the end or target, the good, we "deliberate about and deliberately choose what furthers it" (*NE* 1113[b]3–4). Deliberate choice (*prohairesis*) is thus a matter of choosing (*haireisthai*) one thing before or in preference to (*pro*) another (1112[a]16–17), and so of deliberating about what things should be done *earlier than* or *in preference to* others to further the desired end.

A second reason for locating wish in the rationally calculative part of the soul is that this part would not otherwise be capable of causing action—since without desire of some sort, it cannot do so (*NE* 1139[a]35–36). This would make self-control and lack of self-control (sometimes called weakness of will) difficult to explain, since they seem to presuppose a motivational conflict between appetite or spirit and rational part, which the latter can either lose (lack of self-control) or win (self-control). It is by appeal to such conflict, in any case, that the non-rational components of the desiring part are distinguished from a rational part already conceived as a source of motivation:

> Another natural constituent in the soul [besides the nutritive part] also seems to be non-rational, although it shares in reason in a way. For we praise the reason—that is, the part of the soul that has reason—of a person with self-control and a person without it. For it exhorts them correctly toward what is best. But they also have within them something else besides reason, apparently, which

> fights against reason and resists it. For just as with paralyzed limbs (when their owners deliberately choose to move them to the right, they do the contrary and move off to the left), so it is in the case of the soul as well. For the impulses of people who lack self-control are in contrary directions. In the case of the body, to be sure, we see the part that is moving in the wrong direction, whereas in the case of the soul we do not see it. But presumably we should nonetheless acknowledge that in the soul as well there is something besides reason, countering it and going against it. (*NE* 1102^{b}13–25)

With wish located in the rational part, the way is clear to recognizing a type of *reason* that is distinctively practical, or motivating of action, and a virtue (to which we shall be returning) that is related to both thought and action—namely, practical wisdom (*phronêsis*).

The Ethics of Perception and Understanding

Although not a starting-point of deliberately chosen action (*NE* 1139^{a}19), which is special to adult human beings and requires thought, perception is a starting-point of action in the broader sense of intentional animal movement or behavior. In this regard, a species of it that we may call *action-related* or *"practical"* perception is particularly important:

> [**1**] Perceiving, then, is like bare announcing and understanding (*noein*). [**2**] But when [the perceived object] is pleasant or painful, [the soul], as if affirming or denying, pursues or avoids [the perceived object]. [**3**] In fact, to feel pleasure or pain is to be active with regard to the perceptual mean in relation to what is good or bad, as such. (*DA* 431ᵃ8–12)

When [**1**] we perceive a proper perceptible, we announce its presence, as we announce a guest. When [**2**] what is perceived is pleasant or painful, the soul pursues or avoids it, as if affirming something or denying it, since "what affirmation and denial are in the case of thought, that, in the case of desire, is precisely what pursuit and avoidance are" (*NE* 1139ᵃ21–22). What turns annunciation into affirmation, then, is that an action-causing or movement-causing desire is formed relative to it.

The perceptual mean mentioned in [**3**] is the constituent in a perceptual capacity that functions like a laboratory balance or weighing scale enabling it to detect differences in the special perceptibles that activate it by tilting it, as it were, one way or another (*DA* 424ᵃ5–10). Depending on the makeup of these perceptibles, the activation is either pleasant or painful:

> If voice is a sort of consonance, and voice and hearing are in a way one (while in another way not one and the same), and if consonance is a ratio,

> then hearing must also be a sort of ratio. And that is why each sort of excess, whether high or low pitch, destroys hearing, and similarly excesses in flavor destroy taste, and in colors the intensely bright and dark destroy sight, and in smell the strong odors, whether sweet or bitter, since the perceptual capacity is a sort of ratio. That is also why things—for example, the sharp, sweet, or salty—are pleasant when, being pure and unmixed; they are brought into the ratio, since they are pleasant then. And in general a mixture, a consonance, is more pleasant than either high or low pitch, and for touch what can be [further] heated or cooled. The perceptual capacity is a ratio, and excessive things dissolve or destroy it. (*DA* 426ᵃ27–ᵇ7)

The perception of a special perceptible is pleasant, provided it is within the limits determined by—or consonant with—the structural ratio of the sense (and is painful otherwise).

Perception and pleasure

And the feature of it that makes that actualization pleasant—the relevant good-making feature—is that it is maximally consonant with the ratio that defines or is the sense. **[3]** alerts us to the fact that it is when a sense is activated by a perceptible object with this feature that its being activated constitutes feeling pleasure, or, when the object is discordant with the sense's defining ratio, feeling pain. At the same time, it reminds us that what is being said about pleasure and pain applies also to good and bad generally. For pleasure "accompanies every object of choice" (*NE* 1104^{b}35) and so is woven into every good, as pain into every bad.

The account of perception in **[1–3]** applies to animal action and movement generally, not just to deliberately chosen action. But when the animal in question is a human being possessed of understanding, the account does not stop there:

> **[4]** To the understanding soul, however, appearances are like perceptions. And when it affirms or denies good or bad, it avoids or pursues. That is why the soul never understands without an appearance. **[5]** But just as the air made the eye-jelly be such-and-such, however, and it in turn something else, and hearing likewise, the last thing is one, and a single mean, but the being for it is manifold. (What the thing is by which it discerns that sweet and hot differ has been stated before, but we should also say the following. It is indeed one thing, but in the way a defining mark is, and, since they are one by analogy and in number, it is with respect to each of them as they are with respect to each

other....) [6] The part that understands, then, understands the forms in the appearances, and, as in the previous cases, what is to be pursued or avoided is distinguished for it, and so, even outside of perception, when it is dealing with appearances, it is moved to pursuit or avoidance. For example, [7] perceiving the beacon, because it is fire, by the common [perceptual capacity], seeing it moving, it recognizes that it is the enemy, [8] but sometimes, by means of the appearances or intelligible objects that are in the soul, just as if seeing them, it calculates and deliberates about future things on the basis of present ones. And when it [the soul] says, as it does there, pleasant or painful, here it pursues or avoids—and so in cases of action generally. (DA 431ᵃ14–431ᵇ10)

The goal of the passage is to explain how perception that is related to deliberately chosen action, of the sort relevant, for example, to ethics, is involved in understanding. [4] picks up from [2], explaining that understanding functions in the same way in relation to good or bad that perception does in relation to pleasant and painful. For appearances are structural analogues of perceptions, and so have an effect on understanding similar to the one appearances have on perception. [6] picks up from [3]. The problem, as in the case of the perception of complexes of special perceptibles to which Aristotle refers, is that some mean must discern the sorts of arrays of perceptibles that substances present to practical perception, and thus to understanding. The solution proposed is therefore the same as in the case of perception generally. The mean must be like a limit—a point where many different simpler means, corresponding to each of the senses involved, can meet and register their effects. What is different in this case is just that some constituents of the array will be pleasant or painful, so that understanding, instead of just registering or announcing the presence of the array when activated by it, will do the kind of asserting or denying that is pursuing or avoiding.

Thus far understanding seems to be functioning just like a later stage in perception, but [**6**] alerts us to one way this is not so: understanding, because it makes use of appearances rather than perceptions, can function even "outside of perception," or when perception is not involved. That is one difference. The other is that what understanding understands is not the appearances themselves but the forms that are in them, which are the intelligible objects mentioned in [**8**], which are accessible to understanding only as presented in perceptible ones, or in the appearances that are their structural analogues.

In [**7**] the transition from perception to understanding is direct, in that understanding engages in no explicit reasoning but produces an action directly on the basis of perceptual input and its own extraction of intelligible objects therefrom: in other words, the extraction of the form *enemy* from moving beacons, like a doctor's recognition of some spots as measles, is direct. In [**8**], by contrast, the understanding does engage in explicit calculation or deliberation. Here it uses appearances retained in memory, or the intelligible objects encoded in them, to construct an action-related or "practical" deduction. In this case, pursuit or avoidance follows immediately. Since such actions result from deliberation, [**8**] is the model for how perception and understanding functions in them.

In a text related especially to [**1–3**], Aristotle rejoins the topic of practical perception and understanding:

> This, though, is the way the object of desire and the intelligible object move things: they move them without being moved. Of these objects, the primary ones are the same. For the [primary] object of appetite is the apparently good, and the primary object of wish is the really good. But we desire something because it seems [good] rather than its seeming so because we desire it. For the starting-point is the active understanding. And understanding is moved by intelligible objects. (*Met.* XII 7 1072^{a}26–30)

Understanding is moved by intelligible objects. This movement of understanding is the starting-point of action. For we desire the object in question because it seems a certain way to our understanding, not the other way around. Yet how the object will seem depends on two potentially opposed factors: appetite, which responds to the apparent good, and wish, which responds to the real good. It is when they have done their respective work that a resultant something, which seems a certain way, is produced. It is this—the thing that causes the action—that desire is for. That is why the primary objects of understanding and of desire are the same: what desire is for (or against) is what (as a result of the operations of appetite and wish) seems a certain way to understanding.

What we have in [**1–8**], then, is a somewhat complex picture that is best explained as partly developmental in character. [**1–3**] deals with the perceptual and imaginative precursors of intelligible object, and applies as well to beasts and infants as to mature human adults. Hence what is subsequently presented to understanding soul, in such animals as have it, is [**4**] just what appears to perception, so that it affirms it to be good (pursues) or denies it to be good (avoids) accordingly. At this stage, then, perception, desire, and understanding operate seamlessly, as if they were one thing, so that there is little need to distinguish intelligible objects from the appearances they are encoded in.

Initially, then, perceptible objects control action-related perception, and—in the shape of appearances—understanding. Later on, though, the story is more complex. Now the way things appear to us is a product not of perception alone, but of the various factors that, shaped by habituation and socialization, make up our character:

> Suppose that someone were to say that everyone seeks the apparent good but that we do not control its appearance. Instead, whatever sort of person each of us happens to be also determines the sort of end that appears to him. Well, if each individual is somehow responsible for his own state of character, he is also somehow responsible for the appearance in question. (*NE* 1114^{a}31–^{b}3)

In someone with a virtuous character, these factors work together in such harmony that their separate contributions are all but invisible. In pathological cases, such as that of John, who lacks self-control, the various factors come apart. Bird meat is not salty enough or fatty enough to be consonant with the ratio definitive of John's sense of taste, since that ratio has been skewed by inadequate habituation or bad upbringing to be consonant only with things too salty or fatty to be healthy—a Big Mac, say. To John, therefore, bird meat will appear displeasing. Yet when he has discovered as a result of deliberation that bird meat is what will best further his happiness, the bird meat will be consonant with the mean definitive of his wish. For wish, as we saw, is a desire susceptible to deliberation's outcomes. So his wish will be for the bird meat, since, as lacking self-control, he knows what is good, but does not do it, because his appetite overpowers his wish.

How, then, will the bird meat seem to John's understanding? How will it seem or be represented in the desire—the resultant of appetite and wish—that finally causes John's action? Not as appetite presents it (wholly pleasant), not as wish presents it (not good for you), but as a resultant of the two (pleasant but not good). The greater strength of John's appetite isn't simply a matter of greater oomph or muscle, then. We desire something because it seems good, not the other way around. Hence just how much we desire it—how strong our desire is—is itself to be explained by how good the thing seems. That is why Aristotle can so readily speak of vice or badness as producing "distortion and false views about the starting-points of action" (*NE* 1144^{a}34–36). Vice does not push the true views or better desires out of the way, as a stronger person might elbow aside a weaker one; it distorts how the starting-point of action—the end it aims at—appears to us, much as "distorting" the shape of the eyeball makes one thing look like two (*EE* 1246^{a}28–29). What we must do to our feelings, therefore, to establish a mean in them, that is like the perceptual mean, is correct their distortions, as we do when we correct the distortions in pieces of wood in order to straighten them out (*NE* 1109^{b}6).

Since appearances encode intelligible objects, they have an intelligible structure. So it makes sense to say of the virtue of character that it "teaches *correct belief* about the starting-point" (*NE* 1151^{a}18–19) or that it is the constituent of practical wisdom ensuring "true *supposition*" about the good doable in action (1142^{b}33). Put the other way around, since the relevant intelligible structure is in someone's appearances because he was well brought up under the tutelage of wise adults, its presence there is what the desiring part's "chiming" with the rational one consists in (*NE* 1102^{b}16–28). When an intelligible object approved by reason and wish is the intelligible content of an appearance approved, so to speak, by appetite or spirit, the two are in perfect harmony and agree in everything. This is the mark of the fully virtuous and practically-wise person.

What the developmental story reveals is that even in its earliest stages, desire is consequent on perception of—or appearances of—goodness, not the other way around. It is just that, in those early stages, the difference between the contributions of perception and desire is harder to detect, since the two occur simultaneously. In other words, perceptible objects and appearances play as important a role in the latest stages of development as in the earliest ones, even if these are now much more complex in their mode of generation and subject to different masters, and different conditions of correctness. In the case of pleasant or painful special perceptibles, such as this pleasing shade of red, perception is as effectively inerrant as in the case of red itself. That is the message of [**3**]. This does not mean that our native or untutored perception of either of them is always correct. Senses, as we saw, work properly only in certain conditions and when unimpeded in their operations. Bad light, distance, muddy hues can affect the accuracy of color discernment, as can myopia or cataracts. What the account of action-related perception reveals is that other things, such as appetites not in a mean, can affect it as well.

The mean definitive of sight is naturally tilted in pleasure's favor, so that its range of maximum consonance is incorrect (*NE* 1109ᵇ8–9). As people with an illness are poor discerners of bitter and sweet (1113ᵃ27–29), so children and poorly habituated adults are more pleased than they should be by bright garish colors or very sweet tastes. The task of habituation is to properly compensate for the tilt, relocating the range of maximum consonance in the proper place, or as close to it as possible. Habituation's task is no different when the mean in question is one involved in detecting the complex multi-sense appearance presented by a substantial matter-form compound. The scope of action-related perception, then, is large. Our perceptions and beliefs do not present us with a neutral or value-free world, some parts of which acquire value in our eyes because we already desire them; rather, the things they present to us already include constituents that perforce instill desire, because they are already either pleasant or painful, good or bad.

The ethics of perception

It is these facts about perception, and the influence of desire on it, and of it on desire, that make it possible to speak of perception as having an ethics. More than that, they allow us to see that perception is as fundamental to ethics as it is to more strictly cognitive and theoretical enterprises, such as physics. As forms transmitted as formative movements in the blood are the key to an individual animal's life and persistence, and, as transmitted to offspring, to the continued life of the species, so forms transmitted as formative movements to the perceptual organs and the understanding are the key to ethical and intellectual life.

Understanding

Nous (understanding), whose mode of transmission to offspring we looked at in Chapter 2, must now be looked at again. In the broad sense of the term, someone with *nous* is someone with sound common sense and the cognate verb *noein*, simply means "to think." In the narrow sense, which is the one relevant for us, *nous* (now translated as "understanding") is what makes possible a type of theoretical or contemplative knowledge of universal scientific starting-points (or first principles) that, unlike scientific knowledge in the strict or unconditional sense, is not derived from or justified by anything further. This *nous* is a divine substance (*NE* 1177^{b}19–1178^{a}8)—or anyway the most divine one in us (1177^{a}16)—and, among sublunary animals, is fully possessed only by human beings (1178^{b}24–25).

In operation, we are told, understanding is like "the visual perception of intelligible things" (*Protr.* B24), and it is on vision in particular that Aristotle's account of understanding is modeled. As the eye-jelly must take on the perceptible forms of visible objects without the associated matter in order for seeing to occur, so some constituent of the understanding must take on intelligible forms if active understanding is to occur. This receptive constituent is "passive understanding" (*pathêtikos nous*) (*DA* 430^{a}24–25), which "serves as matter for each kind of thing" (430^{a}10–11) and has a role analogous to that of eye-jelly in the case of visual perception. In addition, there is a productive constituent in understanding, which is "causal and productive, because of producing them all (which, for example, is the role of a craft in relation to its matter)" (430^{a}12–13). This is productive understanding (*nous poiêtikos*) (430^{a}15).

The relationship between productive and passive understanding is explained by analogy with the role of light in color perception: "in fact there is one sort of understanding that is such by becoming all things, while there is another that is such by producing all things in the way that a sort of state, like light, does, since in a way light too makes potential colors into active colors" (*DA* 430ᵃ14–17). For, first, just as light, which is itself a color, is a visible object, so productive understanding is an intelligible one, since "it is capable of understanding through itself" (429ᵇ9). And, second, just as no color is in actuality a color without light, so without productive understanding, passive understanding "understands nothing" (430ᵃ25).

In the following passage, Aristotle expands on this picture:

> **[1]** [Understanding] must, therefore, since it understands all things, be unmixed, in order that it may master them—that is, in order that it may know them. For something foreign intruding into it impedes and obstructs it. **[2]** So too it has no other nature than this, that it is potentially something. That part of the soul, therefore, that is called the understanding (and I mean by the understanding that by which the soul thinks and grasps things) is actively none of the beings before it [actively] understands them. **[3]** That is why it is reasonable that it should not be mixed with the body, since it would then come to be of a certain sort, either cold or hot, or it would have some instrument as the perceptual part does, whereas, as things stand, it has none... **[4]** And it is an intelligible object in just the way its intelligible objects are... (*DA* 429ᵃ18–430ᵃ32)

Because the understanding can **[1]** understand each intelligible form, it must be each of them in potentiality. As a result, [2] the only nature its passive component can have is that very capacity or potential, since if it had an intelligible form of its own, it would be unable to take on any other intelligible form distinct from it. This is similar to the argument that the eye-jelly must be transparent. For essentially the same reason, [3] understanding cannot be mixed with (sublunary) body: if it were already earthy in nature, for example, it could not take on the intelligible form of fire. Moreover, just as a transparent object is visible because of "the color of something else" (*DA* 418^{b}5–6), so [4] passive understanding is intelligible because it can take on the intelligible forms of other things.

In explaining why human beings have a better functioning understanding than other animals, Aristotle appeals not to the nature of the understanding itself, but to material processes in the body:

> Instead of having forelegs and forefeet, the human has arms and so-called hands. For the human is the only animal that stands upright, and this is because its nature, that is, its substance is divine. Now the function of that which is most divine is understanding and thinking; and this would not be easy if there were a great deal of the body at the top weighing it down, for weight hampers the movement of understanding and of the common sense. Thus when the weight and the body-like quality becomes too great, the body itself must

> lurch forward toward the ground; and then, for preservation's sake, nature provides forefeet instead of arms and hands—as has happened in quadrupeds . . . because their soul could not sustain the weight bearing it down . . . In fact, compared with man, all other animals are dwarf-like [that is, top-heavy] . . . That is why all animals are less wise than man. Even among human beings, indeed, children . . . though possessing some other exceptional potentiality, are inferior in the possession of understanding as compared to adults. The cause . . . is that in many of them the starting-point of the soul is movement-hampered and body-like in quality. And if the heat that raises the organism upright wanes still further and the earthly matter waxes, then the animals' bodies also wane, and they will be many-footed; and finally they lose their feet altogether and lie full length on the ground. Proceeding a little further in this way, they actually have their starting-point down below, and finally the head part comes to have neither movement nor sensation and what you have is a plant, which has its upper parts below and its lower parts above. For in plants the roots have the capacity of mouth and head, whereas the seed counts as the opposite, being produced in the upper part of the plant on the ends of the twigs. (*PA* 686ᵃ25–687ᵃ2)

To see more concretely what is going on in the account of understanding, it is useful partly to follow

Aristotle's example by looking at material processes, but also at the scientific knowledge they make possible.

What codes for understanding in all animals that have it, as we saw, is the circular movement of ether. When it is present in an adult human being, equipped with a functioning perceptual system, inductive processes lead to the transmission of forms from perceptible objects to memory, where they are stored, not as actual movements but—as in the case of the movements in female menses—as potential ones. When, as a result of the development of scientific knowledge, these forms become accessible to understanding, memory is transformed into passive understanding. That is why Aristotle can distinguish between perception and understanding in the following way:

> Something is similarly said to be actively perceiving and contemplating. There is the difference, though, that in perception the things productive of the activity are external, namely, what is visible, what is audible, and similarly for the rest of the perceptible objects. The cause of this is that active perception is of particulars, whereas scientific knowledge is of universals, and these are in a way in the soul itself. That is why it is up to us to understand—but not up to us to perceive—whenever we wish, since the perceptible object must be present. (*DA* 417^{b}19–26)

In animals without understanding, or in those, such as children, in which its operations are hampered by processes in the body, this transformation of memory does not take place. Hence they have accesses to stored appearances, but not to their intelligible contents.

What happens when these forms are actively understood is that they touch or come into contact with intrinsically moving ether, which starts them moving, animating them much as pneuma encapsulated in bubbles does their originals in the natural world outside the soul—but with this crucial difference: because what passive understanding takes on is form without matter, what get actualized are just those potentials for movements that realize constituents of the form, not those that realize constituents of the matter. That is why when we understand the form of an elephant, no elephant comes to be in our understanding. But that all this should be experienced as something like having the light go on in one's mind is no easier to explain than the fact that creatures feel pain or see red when certain neurons fire in their brain, or that the actualization of the transparent is experienced as light. Consciousness is often described as the hard problem in the philosophy of mind. Yet we experience our own consciousness as directly and immediately as we experience light when we see. And without it, there would be no science, and, since happiness involves consciousness, no happiness. (Aristotle's ideas about his god, discussed in Chapter 5, are in part a registration of that fact.)

Action-related Understanding

The sort of understanding involved in deliberately chosen action, which is of most importance in ethics, is a variety of it that Aristotle again calls practical (*praktikos*) or action-related:

> Both of these are capable of causing movement with respect to place, namely, understanding and desire—understanding, however, that is of the practical sort, which rationally calculates for the sake of something, and differs from the theoretical sort in respect of the end. And every desire too is for the sake of something. For the object of desire is the starting-point of practical understanding, and the last thing is the starting-point of the action. So it is reasonable that these two things—desire and practical thought—appear to be the causes of movement. For the object of desire moves us, and, because of this, thought causes movement, because its starting-point is the object of desire.... That is why what causes movement in every case is the object of desire, which is either the good or the apparent good—not every good, however, but the good that is doable in action. And what is doable in action is what admits of being otherwise. (*DA* 433ᵃ13–30)

But though practical understanding does have this special sort of role, it is not some new part of the soul distinct from theoretical understanding. Instead—as the passage to some extent suggests—it is more like a combination of theoretical understanding and wish. In this regard, it is analogous to practical perception.

Aristotle is sometimes insistent that theoretical understanding "does not get a theoretical grasp on anything doable in action, and says nothing about what is to be avoided and pursued" (*DA* 432^b27–29). Nonetheless, this does not prevent what it does think about from being coincidentally relevant to action, pursuit, and avoidance in precisely the way scientific knowledge of other sorts can be: "nothing else is the end of astronomy, natural science, or geometry than knowing and having a theoretical grasp on the nature of the things that are the underlying subjects of those sciences—nonetheless, nothing prevents them from being coincidentally useful to us for many of the necessities of life" (*EE* 1216^b11–16). It is theoretical science that tells us that smoking causes lung cancer, that a Mediterranean diet is a healthy one, or that the climate is warming. But with our own good in view, these are useful bits of knowledge for us to have, provided we have the practical wisdom needed to act on them.

But strictly theoretical understanding has practical relevance of a yet more important sort. The verb *theôrein*, which often means "look at" with the eyes, also means "contemplate" with the mind or "have theoretical knowledge" of it. The cognate adjective *theôrêtikos* presents related problems. When applied to a type of life (*NE* 1095^{b}19) or activity (1177^{a}18), it is usually translated as "contemplative." When applied to a type of scientific knowledge or thought, on the other hand, it is usually translated as "theoretical," as opposed to "practical" (*praktikos*). While in many ways apt, this opposition is also somewhat misleading. For what makes something *praktikos* for Aristotle is that it is appropriately related to *praxis* or action, considered as an end choiceworthy because of itself, and not—as with our term "practical"—that it is opposed to what is theoretical, speculative, or ideal. Hence, though it sounds odd to our ears, *theôrêtikos* activities are more *praktikos* than those that are widely considered to be most so:

> Yet it is not necessary, as some suppose, for an action-involving life to be lived in relation to other people, nor are those thoughts alone action-involving that arise for the sake of the consequences of doing an action, rather, much more so are the acts of contemplation and thought that are their own ends and are engaged in for their own sake. For doing well in action is the end, and so action of a sort is the end too. (*Pol.* 1325^{b}16–21) .

Theoretical and practical

If some things are *praktikos*, because, like practical ones, they are useful, effective, or feasible means to some end, others are yet more praktikos because they further an end by constituting it or being identical to it: "we put both health and wealth among the things doable in action, and also the things we do for the sake of these, namely, health-producing and wealth-acquiring ones), it is clear that happiness too must be put down as the best for a human being of the things doable in action" (*EE* 1217^a37–40). Means to ends are practical, but so—preeminently—are the ends themselves.

So even though theoretical wisdom (*sophia*) does not "contemplate any of the things from which a human being will come to be happy (for it is not concerned with anything coming-to-be)" (*NE* 1143^b19–20), since it is itself what complete happiness involves, it is much more practical even than the practical wisdom that does contemplate them. The dramatic ethical consequences of this will be further explored in Chapter 4.

Chapter 4

Human Beings and Their Happiness

Form and function

A thing's function is intimately related to its nature, form, and essence. For a thing's nature is its end (*Ph.* 194ª27–28), its form is more its nature than its matter (193ᵇ6–7), and its essence and form are the same (*Met.* 1032ᵇ1–2). Hence "all things are defined by their function" (*Mete.* 390ª10), with the result that if something cannot function, it has no more than a name in common with its functional self (*Pol.* 1253ª20–25). Functions are thus attributed to a wide variety of things, whether living or non-living. These include plants (*GA* 731ª24–26) and animals generally (*NE* 1176ª3–5), parts of their bodies and souls (*PA* 686ª26–29), instruments or tools of various sorts (*EE* 1242ª15–19), as well as crafts, sciences (1219ª17), and their practitioners (*NE* 1141ᵇ10).

But instead of arguing directly that human beings as such have a function, he treats the uncontroversial fact that craftsmen have "certain functions and actions," and that bodily parts, such as eyes, hands, and feet do (1097^{b}28–33), as making it absurd to think that human beings do not have one. The first thought seems to be that if in his role as a craftsman of various sorts a human being has a function, he must also have a function of a more general type that suits him to play those roles, and to adapt himself to the rational principles and norms of the associated crafts and sciences. A chef must follow a recipe, a musician must be able to follow a score. Since human beings are able to be both chefs and musicians they must have the more abstract capacity enabling them, with suitable training, to be able to follow both recipes and scores. The second thought seems to reach the same conclusion by something like the reverse route: if each part of the human body has a function, the whole of which they are the parts must also have one, to which each of theirs contributes, so that its function explains theirs.

Whatever the human function turns out to be, then, it must be something we can intelligibly think of as explaining the functions of the parts of the human body, and how it is that human beings can be craftsmen of various sorts, subject to the rational principles or norms of their craft. These are the requirements that shape Aristotle's search (boldface numerals will again help us keep track of its various steps and stages):

> **[1]** What, then, could this [human function] be? For living (*zên*) is evidently shared with plants as well, but we are looking for what is special. Hence we must set aside the living that consists in nutrition and growth. Next in order is some sort of perceptual living. But this too is evidently shared with horse and ox and every animal. **[2]** There remains, then, some sort of practical living of the part that has reason. And of what has reason, **[3]** one part has it by dint of obeying reason, the other by dint of actually having it and exercising thought. **[4]** But "living" is said of things in two ways, and we must take the one in accord with activity, since it seems to be called "living" in a fuller sense. (*NE* 1097^{b}33–1098^{a}7)

Zôê refers to the sorts of life processes studied by biologists, zoologists, and other scientists: growth and reproduction are such processes, as are perceiving and understanding. As a result it is, as **[4]** tells us, ambiguous, referring either to the potential to grow, reproduce, or perceive, or to the process or activity of growing, reproducing, perceiving, or understanding. A second word, *bios*, refers to the sort of life a natural historian or (auto)biographer might investigate—the life of the otter, the life of Pericles—and so to a span of time throughout which someone possesses *zôê* as a potential, something they can do even when asleep (*NE* 1102^{b}5–7). Hence we are later reminded that a *zôê* will not be happiness for a human being unless it occurs "in a complete *bios*" (1098ᵃ18–20).

What is characterized as "practical" in [**2**] is the *zôê* of what possesses reason, which might lead us to think that what is being referred to is a peculiarly practical as opposed to theoretical or contemplative rational activity. But what is practical, as we saw at the end of Chapter 3, often includes what is theoretical or contemplative, rather than excluding it. [**3**] seems intended to remind us of just this fact. Rational activity, it tells us, is twofold—that of the part that obeys reason, which is the desiring part, and that of the part that possesses reason autonomously, which comprises, the deliberative part, the scientific part, and the understanding (*NE* 1139ᵃ3–15). But when we consider the desiring part, in the way that [**4**] requires, as actively obeying reason, it also involves the activity of the deliberative calculative subpart of the part that possesses reason autonomously. The twofold activity of what possesses reason is thus active desiring in accord with practical thinking or deliberation and theoretical thinking or contemplation. It is this that paves the way for the disjunctive conclusion of the argument as a whole: "the human good turns out to be activity of soul in accord with virtue, and, if there are more virtues than one, in accord with the best and most complete" (1098ᵃ16–18).

The implicit argument by elimination that Aristotle uses in [**1–2**] to identify the human function with rational activity of a sort presupposes the account of the soul we looked at in Chapter 3. But whichever account of we appeal to, rational activity of some sort is likely to emerge as best fitted for the double explanatory duty the human function must perform. For the crafts and sciences are rational enterprises, and the parts of the body, since they can be moved in accord with their norms—as a violinist can move her hands so as to play the notes in the score she is following—are arguably adapted by nature to serve for this purpose:

> But since every instrument is for the sake of something, and each of the parts of the body is for the sake of something, and what they are for the sake of is a sort of action, it is evident that the whole body too has been composed for the sake of a certain complete action. For sawing is not for the sake of the saw, but the saw for that of sawing. For sawing is a certain use. So the body too is in a way for the sake of the soul, and the parts for that of the functions for which each has naturally grown. (*PA* 645^{b}14–20)

That is why the human function, as a rational activity of the soul, is something beyond the functions of the bodily parts (*NE* 1097^{b}32–33).

When something has a function, moreover, there is always some virtue or excellence (*aretê*) that enables it to perform that function well: "every virtue, regardless of what thing it is the virtue of, both completes the good state of that thing and makes it perform its function well" (*NE* 1106^{a}15–17). By the same token, there is some vice (*kakia*) that causes the function to be performed badly. Once the human function is identified with a type of rational activity, then, the virtues that ensure its good performance are automatically on the scene as well:

> [5] If, then, the function of a human being is activity of the soul in accord with reason or not without reason, and the function of a sort of thing, we say, is the same in kind as the function of an excellent thing of that sort (as in the case of a lyre player and an excellent lyre player), and this is unconditionally so in all cases when we add to the function the superiority that is in accord with the virtue (for it is characteristic of a lyre player to play the lyre and of an excellent one to do it well)—if all this is so, and a human being's function is supposed to be a sort of living, and this living is supposed to be activity of the soul and actions that involve reason, and it is characteristic of an excellent man to do these well and nobly, and each is completed well when it is in accord with the virtue that properly belongs to it— if all this is so, the human good turns out to be activity of the soul in accord with virtue and, if there are more virtues than one, then in accord with the best and most complete. (*NE* 1098^{a}7–20)

Aristotle's investigation of happiness can then focus on the various candidate virtues governing rational activity, with the aim of discovering which of them is most complete.

If activity in accord with the most complete virtue is to constitute complete happiness, however, it must receive "a complete span of life (*bios*)" (*NE* 1177[b]25) or must occur in or throughout "a complete life (*bios*)" (1098[a]18). But what exactly is a complete life? We might think that it is one of normal length—three scores years and ten, or whatever. But the completeness assigned to a life in the *Nicomachean Ethics* cannot be of this sort, since what is said there about virtue seems plainly inconsistent with it:

> It is true of an excellent [or fully virtuous] person too that he does many actions for the sake of his friends and his fatherland, even dying for them if need be. For he will give up wealth, honors, and fought-about goods generally, in keeping for himself what is nobly beautiful (*kalon*). For he will choose intense pleasure for a short time over weak pleasure for a long one; living life in a nobly beautiful way for a year over many years lived in random fashion; and a single nobly beautiful and great action over many small ones. This is presumably what happens with those who die for others. (*NE* 1169[a]18–25)

It may be true, of course, that a happy life is presumptively of normal length, provided we recognize that a shorter life can also be happy if its shortness is compensated for in some way.

The sort of life (*bios*) to which a natural life expectancy belongs, indeed, is primarily a biological life: elephants and plants also have life expectancies in this sense. But an individual human being's life, as we saw, is also an (auto-) biographical life, which can be a success—can be worthwhile and in need of nothing—even if it is not of normal length. One way it might be so is by containing, like the life of a great hero, "a single action that is nobly beautiful and grand"—that is to say, an action of the sort the *Iliad* or *Odyssey* is built around, "an action that is unified, and a whole as well, whose parts, consisting of the events that happen, so constructed that the displacement or removal of any one of them will disturb and disjoint the whole" (*Po.* 1451^{a}32–35). (We might think of the plot of such a story as the form that is transmitted to the actions that the story describes.) Such a life may in a way be of normal length, but what is really important is that by achieving a good end it is complete.

The human function

In one way it is easy to say what the human function is: it is **[5]** activity of the soul in accord with reason. It is when we try to be more specific that we run into difficulties. For there seem to be various possibilities for what such activity could be. It could, for example, be some sort of contemplative activity of the sort that theoretical wisdom completes or perfects, or it could be practical activity of the sort that practical wisdom and the virtues of character (such as courage and justice) perfect, or it could be some sort of activity involving reason that all of these virtues together somehow perfect.

In the *Protrepticus*, we find Aristotle apparently confronting this problem in an interesting way, unparalleled in his other works:

> **[6]** When each thing completes in the best way that which—not coincidentally but intrinsically—is its function, the thing in question must be said to be good too, and the virtue by which each thing can by nature accomplish this should be deemed to have the most control. What is composite and divisible into parts has several different activities, but what is by nature simple and does not have its substance in relation to something else must have one controlling virtue intrinsically. If then a human being is a simple animal and his substance is ordered in accord both with reason and with understanding, he has no other function than this alone, namely, the attainment of the most exact truth about the beings. But if he is naturally co-composed of several capacities, and it is clear that he has by nature several functions to be completed, the best of them is always his function, as health

> is the function of the doctor, and safety of a ship's captain. (B63–65)

[6] tells us, in a way with which we are already familiar, that a thing's function is what the virtue with most control (the most complete virtue) completes or perfects, and contrasts two kinds of beings: a simple being—the god (discussed in Chapter 5)—who has only one function, and so only one virtue, and a complex being with many parts. If a human being were a simple animal, his function would be "the attainment of the most exact truth." But he is not a simple animal. Instead, he has many potentialities and functions to be completed, and so (by implication) many virtues too. Nonetheless, it is the best of these functions that is *his* function, so that the virtue that perfects or complete it will be his most complete virtue.

To take the next step we need first to acknowledge complexity in Aristotle's use of the term *anthrôpos*—or in his conception of what a human being is. While *anthrôpos* often does refer to the whole human animal, composed of body and soul, it sometimes refers to the (merely) human element in human beings by contrast with the divine one:

> But such a [contemplative] life would be more excellent than one in accord with the human element (*anthrôpon*), since it is not insofar as he is a human being (*anthrôpos*) that someone will live a life like that but insofar as he has some divine

element in him, and to the degree that this element is superior to the compound, to that degree will its activity also be superior to that in accord with the other sort of virtue. (*NE* 1177[b]26–29)

But sometimes, as we are about to see, it refers to that divine element itself, since it is what makes human beings distinctively human. Thus when we ask what the special function of a human being is, we need to be clear about what we think a human being is. And here is Aristotle telling us what he takes the answer to be:

[7] For each human being, then, the life in accord with understanding is so too, if indeed this most of all is a human being. Hence, this life will also be happiest. (*NE* 1178[a]6–8)

And the proper way to understand it is indicated in the following text:

[8] A person is called "self-controlled" or "lacking in self-control" depending on whether or not his understanding is in control, on the supposition that this is what each person is, and it is actions involving reason that people seem most of all to do themselves and to do voluntarily. So it is clear enough that this part is what each person is or is most of all and that a decent person likes this part most. (*NE* 1168[b]34–1169[a]2)

It follows that [7] is every bit as much about control as it is about identity.

The real self

Now, when contemporary philosophers try to understand human agency, they often find themselves wanting to distinguish actions that originate in—or have their causal source in—the agent from actions that stem from the agent's "real self" or "will" or what the agent "identifies" with. A reforming smoker, for example, may succumb to temptation and exhibit lack of self-control by smoking a cigarette, without thereby returning to being a smoker. Why? Because that action stems from a desire that is no longer a part of his true self, no longer part of his will or what he identifies with. However precisely we are best to understand the psychology of agency that makes these distinctions fully intelligible, it is attractive to see Aristotle as making an early contribution to it, since this allows us to make good sense of [7]. For on this way of looking at them degrees of identity have no place in them. We are most of all our understanding because our understanding is our "true self"—the source of those actions that are most our own, that we most identify with. And our function—even though unlike the god we are complex beings—is our function for the same reason. It is, so to speak, the function that is most of all ours—the function of what we most of all identify with.

It no surprise, then, that the one significant piece of practical advice in the *Nicomachean Ethics* is this:

> One must not, however, in accord with the makers of proverbs, "think human things (*anthrôpina*), since you are human" or "think mortal things, since you are mortal" but, rather, one must as far as possible immortalize, and do everything to live in accord with the element in us that is most excellent. (*NE* 1177ᵇ31–33)

For if a human being really is his understanding, his happiness and its happiness must surely be the same thing. So the question now is, what does happiness consist in for his understanding, what must he understand, what must he contemplate, in order to be happy? Well, as we saw, "every virtue, regardless of what thing it is the virtue of, both completes the good state of that thing and makes it perform its function well" (*NE* 1106ᵃ15–17), contemplation is *the* function of human beings, and theoretical wisdom is the virtue that ensures that contemplation is performed well (1144ᵃ2). And it is performed well, the following text tells us, if it meets three condition:

> The theoretically-wise person must not only know what follows from the starting-points but must also grasp the truth where the starting-points are concerned. So theoretical

> wisdom would be understanding plus scientific knowledge—scientific knowledge, having a head as it were, of the most estimable things. (*NE* 1141ᵃ17–20)

Just what it is to meet these conditions, and what the most estimable things are, we are about to find out.

Chapter 5

Science, Dialectic, and God

It is clear from the beginning that the distinctive focus of *De Caelo* or *On the Heavens* is not primarily or exclusively on the world of sublunary nature (*phusis*), which consists canonically of matter-form compounds, whose material component involves the sublunary elements (earth, water, air, and fire), but on the superlunary or *super*-natural realm, *ho ouranos* ("the heaven"), as Aristotle calls it, consisting of celestial spheres, composed of primary body or ether (*Cael.* 270^{b}21), as well as the stars and planets affixed to them. Nonetheless, if its scope is more catholic than a strictly natural science, much of what it discusses (for example, the sublunary elements, heaviness and lightness, up and down) has obvious application in the sublunary realm. In any case, and perhaps most tellingly, the evidentiary basis of the science exemplified in *De Caelo* science is perceptual and empirical: "what appears to be so to perception has the controlling vote in every case" (*Cael.* $306^{a}17$). That is why it is "experience in astronomy" that must provide the starting-points of astronomical science (*APr.* $46^{a}19$–20).

It could hardly be clearer that however we are to conceive of the super-natural it cannot be as a realm entirely different in kind from the natural one. Super-nature, to put it this way, is a sort of nature, not a sort of something else. Similarly, in *On Coming to Be and Passing Away*, *De Caelo*'s immediate predecessor, we are reminded that the discussion must be conducted *phusikôs*—in a way appropriate to natural science ($316^{a}11$, $335^{b}25$) and that perception is not something reason (theory) should overstep or disregard ($325^{a}13$–14), but should be in agreement with our arguments ($336^{b}15$–17). Indeed, if it fails in this regard, it is reason that must go:

> On the basis of reason (*logos*), then, and on the basis of what seem to be the facts about them, matters having to do with generation of bees appear to be this way. The facts, though, have certainly not been sufficiently grasped, but if at some time they are, one should take perception rather than reasonings to be what must carry

> conviction, and reasonings [only] if what they show agrees with what appears to be the case. (*GA* 760ᵇ27–33)

The lab, to be anachronistic, not the armchair, has pride of place, even if there is also much that can be done in that more cozy place: "We consider that we have adequately demonstrated in accord with reason (*logos*) things unapparent to perception if we have led things back to what is possible" (*Mete.* 344ᵃ5–7). This has obvious application not just to astronomical objects inaccessible in the absence of telescopes, but to cellular structure, genes, DNA, and the like that are similarly inaccessible in the absence of microscopes.

Now if the various bodies, natural and supernatural, were the only substances, the only primary beings, the science of them would be the science that the *Metaphysics* proposes to investigate, and refers to indifferently as theoretical wisdom (*sophia*) (982ᵃ2), theological philosophy (1026ᵃ19), and the science of being insofar as it is being. That there is a substance (a divine one indeed) that is eternal and immovable is argued in *Physics* Book VIII, and presupposed in *On Coming to Be and Passing Away* Book II Chapter 10. But there is a problem about its very possibility.

Aristotle usually divides the bodies of knowledge he refers to as *epistêmai* ("sciences") into three types: theoretical, practical, and productive (crafts). When he is being especially careful, he also distinguishes within the theoretical sciences between the strictly theoretical ones (astronomy, theology), as we may call them, and the natural ones, which are like the strictly theoretical ones in being neither practical nor productive but unlike them in consisting of propositions that—though necessary and universal in some sense—hold for the most part rather than without exception:

> If all thought is either practical or productive or theoretical, natural science would have to be some sort of theoretical science—but a theoretical science that is concerned with such being as is capable of being moved and with the substance that in accord with its account holds for the most part only, because it is not separable [from sublunary matter]. (*Met.* 1025^{b}25–28)

Psychology, as a result, has an interestingly mixed status, part strictly theoretical, because it deals with understanding, which is something divine, part natural, because it deals with perception and memory and other capacities that require a body (*DA* 403^{a}25–^{b}16). Psychology has a theological dimension, then, as well as a more naturalistic biological or psychological one. Indeed, biology, at any rate when with the transmission of understanding from progenitor to offspring, itself has a foot, so to speak, in the supernatural, as we saw in Chapter 1.

With all this before us, we are in a position to say something further about the science of *De Caelo*. That it is not a work of strictly natural science, but rather of super-natural science, we know. That it is theoretical rather than productive or practical is plain. But what sort of theoretical science is it exactly? Insofar as it is a work of astronomy (or what we would probably call cosmology), we know at least where Aristotle himself puts it, since he refers to astronomy as "the mathematical science that is most akin to philosophy" (*Met.* 1073^{b}4–5). Yet it is not a branch of pure mathematics but rather something closer to what we would call applied mathematics:

> Odd and even, straight and curved, and furthermore number, line, and figure will be without movement, whereas flesh, bone, and human will not, but rather all of them are said of things just as snub nose is and not as curved is. This is also clear from the more natural-science-like parts of mathematics, such as optics, harmonics, and astronomy. For these are in a way the reverse of geometry. For whereas geometry investigates natural lines, but not insofar as they are natural, optics investigates mathematical lines, but not insofar as they are mathematical. (*Ph.* 194^{a}3–12)

A mathematical science, then, but a more natural-scientific one than one pure or abstract.

At the same time, Aristotle tell us too that while we think about "the stars as bodies only, that is, as units having a certain order, altogether inanimate," we should in fact "conceive of them as participating in action and life" (*Cael.* 292^{a}18–21) and of their action as being "like that of animals and plants" (292^{b}1–2). And the complexity does not end there. For he also includes the primary heaven, the sphere of the fixed stars, as among things divine:

> The activity of a god is immortality, and this is eternal living. So it is necessary that eternal movement belong to the god. And since the heaven is such (for it is a certain divine body), because of this it has a circular body, which by nature always moves in a circle. (*Cael.* 286^{a}9–12)

Thus the science to which *De Caelo* contributes is apparently at once a natural-scientific branch of mathematics, a biological science, and a theological one. It also makes clear that the god referred to (the *primary god* as we may call him) is only one, though the most important and estimable one, of the divine beings.

Aristotelian science

When science receives its focused discussion in the *Nicomachean Ethics*, however, Aristotle is explicit that if we are "to speak in an exact way and not be guided by mere similarities" (1139^{b}19), we should not call anything a science unless it deals with eternal, entirely exception-less facts about universals that are wholly necessary and do not at all admit of being otherwise (1139b20–21). Since he is here explicitly epitomizing his more detailed discussion of science in the *Posterior Analytics*, we should take the latter too as primarily a discussion of science in the exact sense, which it calls *epistêmê haplôs*—unconditional scientific knowledge. It follows that only the strictly theoretical sciences are sciences in this sense. It is on these that the others should be modeled to the extent that they can: "it is the things that are always in the same state and never undergo change that we must make our basis when pursuing the truth, and this is the sort of thing that the heavenly bodies are" (1063a13–15). Having made the acknowledgment, though, we must also register the fact that Aristotle himself mostly does not speak in the exact way but instead persistently refers to bodies of knowledge other than the strictly theoretical sciences as *epistêmai*. His division of the epistêmai into theoretical, practical, and productive is a dramatic case in point.

An Aristotelian science is a state of the soul—a state of the scientist—that involves an affirmational grasp of a set of true propositions (*NE* 1139b14–16). Some of these propositions are indemonstrable starting-points or first principles (*archai*), which are, or are expressed in, definitions, and others are theorems demonstrable from these starting-points. We can have scientific knowledge only of the theorems, since—exactly speaking—only what is demonstrable can be scientifically known. Yet—in what is clearly another lapse from exact speaking—Aristotle characterizes theoretical wisdom as the *epistêmê* that provides "a theoretical grasp of the primary starting-points and causes" (*Met.* 982b7–10).

Now it is a cliché of the history of philosophy that Aristotle is an empiricist and Plato a rationalist, and as is the case with all clichés there is some truth in it. In fact, Aristotle is not just an empiricist at the level of the sciences we call empirical, he is an empiricist at all levels. To see what I mean, think of each of the sciences—the *first-order* sciences—as giving us a picture of a piece of the universe, a region of being. Then ask, what is the universe like that these sciences collectively portray? What is the nature of reality as a whole—of being as a whole? If there is no answer besides the collection of special answers, the universe is, as Aristotle puts is, episodic—like a bad tragedy (*Met.* 1076a1, 1090b20). But if there is an answer, it should emerge from a meta-level empirical investigation of the first-order sciences themselves. As each of these looks for universals (natural kinds) that stand in demonstrative causal relations to each other, so this meta-level investigation looks for higher-level universals that reveal the presence of common structures of explanation in diverse sciences:

> The causes and starting-points of distinct things are distinct in a way, but in a way—if we are to speak

> universally and analogically—they are the same for all... For example, the elements of perceptible bodies are presumably: as *form*, the hot and, in another way, the cold, which is the *lack* [of form]; and, as *matter*, what is potentially these directly and intrinsically. And both these and the things composed of them are substances, of which these are the starting-points (that is, anything that comes to be from the hot and the cold that is one [something-or-other], such as flesh or bone), since what comes to be from these must be distinct from them. These things, then, have the same elements and starting-points (although distinct things have distinct ones). But that all things have the same ones is not something we can say just like that, although *by analogy* they do. That is, we might say that there are three starting-points—the form and the lack and the matter. But each of these is distinct for each category—for example, in colors they are white, black, and surface, or light, darkness, and air, out of which day and night come to be. (*Met.* 1070ᵃ31–ᵇ21)

The first-order sciences show the presence in the universe of a variety of *different* explanatory structures. The higher-order sciences, by finding commonalities between these structures, show the equally robust presence there of the *same* explanatory structure: form, lack of form, matter.

The science to which form, lack of form, and matter belong is, in the first instance, higher-order or universal natural science, which is the one of which biology, for example, is a part. Natural science is the one that would be the primary science, as we saw, were there no eternal immovable substances separable from the natural ones. But there is also a higher-order—or universal—mathematical science:

> We might raise a puzzle indeed as to whether the primary philosophy is universal or concerned with a particular genus and one particular nature. For it is not the same way even in the mathematical sciences, but rather geometry and astronomy are concerned with a particular nature, whereas universal mathematics is common to all. (*Met.* 1026^{a}23–27)

The introduction of intelligible matter (*Met.* 1036^{a}11–12), as the matter of abstract mathematical objects, allows us to see a commonality in explanatory structure between the mathematical sciences and the natural ones. Between these two higher-order sciences and the theological one (1026^{a}19), on the other hand, the point of commonality lies not in matter, since the objects of theological science have no matter (1071^{b}20–21), but rather in form. For what the objects of theology, namely, divine substances (which include the human understanding or *nous*), have in common with those of mathematics and natural science is that they are forms, though—and this is the crucial point of difference—not forms in any sort of matter whatsoever.

Form and the science of being insofar as it is being

That form should be a focal topic of investigation for the science of being insofar as it is being is thus the result of an inductive or empirical investigation of the various first-order sciences, and then of the various higher-order ones, which shows form to be the explanatory feature common to all their objects—to all beings.

It is a nice question, but one now within reach of an answer, as to how the science of *De Caelo* is to be incorporated into this uniform explanatory structure. But it is perhaps enough to notice that its objects of study are matter-form compounds, like those of natural science, but with this one difference: their matter is primary body (ether) rather than earth, water, fire, and air in some combination or other. And because the difference this makes is that astronomical objects, though in many cases biological, are amenable to being studied by an applied mathematical science, it must be that primary body is relevantly similar to intelligible matter. It must be like it in not deforming geometrical shapes, unlike it in being concrete rather than abstract: a sphere made of earth (say) cannot be a perfect sphere; a sphere made of primary body can. Result: the heavenly bodies are perfect or exact models of geometrical theorems, while sublunary bodies are no better than imperfect ones. Hence the need to take account of the margin of error. (Recall the case of embryology where potential movements in the female menses can distort male form with the dramatic result that the offspring may be female rather than male.) Thus super-natural science of *De Caelo* variety enters the uniform explanatory structure required for the existence of the science of being insofar as it is being by doors already opened by natural and mathematical science.

It is all this that provides the science of being insofar as it is being with a genuine object of study, thereby legitimating it as every bit as much a science as any first-order one. The science of being insofar as it is being is accordingly a science of form. The question now is how can that science at the same time be theology, the science of divine substance? And to it Aristotle gives the succinct answer that we have already noticed:

> If there is some immovable substance, this [that is, theological philosophy] will be prior and will be primary philosophy, and it will be universal in this way, namely, because it is primary. And it will belong to it to get a theoretical grasp on being insofar as it is being, both what it is and the things that belong to it insofar as it is being. (*Met.* 1026^{a}23–32)

So the primacy of theology, which is based on the fact that theology deals with substance that is eternal, immovable, and separable, is supposedly what justifies us in treating it as the universal science of being insofar as it is being.

To get a handle on what this primacy is, we need to turn to being and its structure. The first thing to grasp is that beings are divided into categories: substance, quality, quantity, relation, time, place, and so on. (These are studied, appropriately enough, in the treatise we call *Categories*.) But of these, only beings in the category of substance are separable, so that they alone enjoy a sort of ontological priority that is both existential and explanatory. Thus walking and being healthy are characterized as "incapable of being separated," on the grounds that there is some particular substantial underlying subject of which they are predicated (*Met.* 1028^a20–31). And often, indeed, separability is associated with being such a subject: "The underlying subject is prior, which is why the substance is prior" (1019^a5–6); "If we do not posit substances to be separated, and in the way in which particular things are said to be separated, we will do away with the sort of substance we wish to maintain" (1086^b16–19). Similarly, not being separable is associated with being predicated of such a subject: "All the other things are either said of the primary substances as subjects or in them as subjects. So if the primary substances were not, it would be impossible for any of the other things to be" (*Cat.* 2^b3–6).

If we want to explain, then, what a quality is, we have to say what sort of attribute it is, and ultimately what in a substance is receptive of it. It is this fact that gives one sort of unity to beings: they are all either substances or attributes of substances. Hence the famous claim:

> Indeed, the question that was asked long ago, is now, and always will be asked, and is always raising puzzles—namely, What is being?—is just the question, What is substance? . . . And that is why we too must most of all, primarily, and (one might almost say) exclusively get a theoretical grasp on what it is that is a being in this [substantial] way. (*Met.* 1028^{b}2–7)

The starting-points and causes of the beings insofar as they are beings, then, must be substances. Thus while things are said to be in as many ways as there are categories, they are all so-said "with reference to one thing and one nature" (*Met.* 1003^{a}33–34)—substance. It could still be the case, of course, that the universe is episodic like a bad tragedy, made up of lots of separate substances having little ontologically to do with each other, but the number of episodes has at least been systematically reduced.

Before turning to the next phase in being's unification, we need to look more closely at substance itself as it gets investigated and analyzed in *Metaphysics* Books VII–IX. The analysis begins with a *legomenon*—with something said and accepted quite widely.

> Something is said to be (*legetai*) substance, if not in more ways, at any rate most of all in four. For the essence, the universal, and the genus seem to be the substance of each thing, and fourth of these, the underlying subject. (*Met.* 1028^b33–36)

Since "the primary underlying subject seems most of all to be substance" (*Met.* 1029^a1–2), because what is said or predicated of it depends on it, the investigation begins with this subject, quickly isolating three candidates: the matter, the compound of matter and form, and the form itself (1029^a2–3), which is identical to essence (1032^b1–2). Almost as quickly (1029^a7–32), the first two candidates are at least provisionally excluded. A—perhaps *the*—major ground for their exclusion is the *primacy dilemma*, which we shall now quickly investigate.

The philosophical background to the dilemma is this. If you are a realist about scientific knowledge and truth, as Aristotle is, the structure of your scientific theories must mirror the structure of reality, so that scientific starting-points or first principles, must also be the basic building blocks of reality. Suppose that this is not so. Suppose that your physics tells you that atoms are the basic building blocks of reality and that your psychology tells you that sense-perceptions are the starting-points of scientific knowledge. Then you will face a very severe problem—that of skepticism. For a wedge can be driven between the starting-points of scientific knowledge and reality's basic building blocks. René Descartes' famous dreaming argument is one familiar form such a wedge might take. Your sense-perceptions are consistent with your being always asleep and having a very detailed dream. Alternatively, an evil neuroscientist could be stimulating your brain so as to make it seem to you as if you are in a world like ours, when in fact your brain is in a vat in a world very different from ours, which your scientific theories do not fit at all. There atoms are not the fundamental building blocks.

Here now is Aristotle raising his version of this very problem:

> We must ... ask whether [the starting-points] are universal or exist in the way we say particulars do. For if they are universal, they will not be substances. For no common thing signifies a this something but a such-and-such sort of thing, whereas substance is a this something.... If then the starting-points are universals, these things follow. But if they are not universals, but [exist] as particulars, they will not be scientifically knowable. For scientific knowledge of all things is universal. Thus there will be other starting-points prior to the starting-points, namely, those that are predicated universally, if indeed there is going to be scientific knowledge of these. (*Met.* 1003[a]7–17)

The basic building blocks of reality, (Aristotelian) science tells us, are particular matter-form compounds—you, me, this oak tree, that cat, and so on. Yet science's own starting-points are the forms—the universal essences of such things. There is no science of you, or of me, but there is one of human beings. How, then, can science possible be reflecting accurately the structure of reality, when its starting-points and those of reality fail so radically to map onto each other? For there is no greater difference, it seems, than that between particulars and universals. The thing to do, then, given that science provides our best access to the nature of reality, is to investigate the universal forms or essences that are basic to it.

Aristotle begins the investigation with the most familiar and widely recognized case, which is the form or essence present in sublunary matter-form compounds. It is announced in *Metaphysics* Book VII Chapter 3 (1029^b3–12), but not begun till some chapters later and not really completed till the end of Book IX Chapter 5. And, by then it is with actuality (*entelecheia*) or activity (*energeia*) that form is identified, and matter with potentiality.

Activity and actuality

The term *energeia* is an Aristotelian coinage, translated as "activity." The etymology of the coinage is unclear, but Aristotle is explicit that it has been extended from movement to other things (*Met.* 1046^a1–2, 1047^a30–32), and that it is related to another term with an erg- root, and one we have already encountered, namely, *ergon* ("function"): "The function is the end, and the activity is the function, and that is why the name 'activity' is said of things with reference to the function and extends to the actuality (*entelecheian*)" (1050ᵃ21–23). *Entelecheia* is also an Aristotelian coinage. It is mostly used as a synonym of *energeia*, but with a slightly different connotation: *energeia* is action, activity, and movement oriented; *entelecheia*—as the *tel-* suggests—is end or telos or completion (enteles) oriented (1021ᵇ24–30). Putting all this together: the activation or actualization of X is an activity, which is X active or actual, which is X achieving its end, which—since "the end is the function" (996ᵇ7)—is X fulfilling its function, and being actively or actually X, and so being complete.

Precisely because actuality and potentiality are the ultimate explanatory factors, however, they themselves cannot be given an explanatory definition in yet more basic terms. Instead, we must grasp them by means of an analogy:

> What we wish to say is clear from the particular cases by induction, and we must not look for a definition of everything, but be able to comprehend the analogy, namely, that as what is building is in relation to what is capable of building, and what is awake is in relation to

> what is asleep, and what is seeing is in relation to what has its eyes closed but has sight, and what has been shaped out of the matter is in relation to the matter, and what has been finished off is to the unfinished. Of the difference exemplified in this analogy let the activity be marked off by the first part, the potentiality by the second. (*Met.* 1048[a]35–[b]6)

What is common to matter-form compounds, mathematical objects, and divine substances, then, is actuality. In the case of matter-form compounds and numbers, the actuality is accompanied by potentiality—perceptual sublunary matter in the first case, intelligible matter in the second. In the case of divine substances and other such unmoved movers, it is not. They are "pure" activities or actualities, wholly actual at each moment, with no potential of theirs left unactualized, or to be actualized in the future. Matter-form compounds, by contrast, are never wholly actual—they always involve some unactualized potential. You are actually reading this now, not reading the newspaper, but you could be reading the newspaper, since you have the presently un-actualized capacity (or potential) to read it. Once you were a fertilized ovum, now you are an adult human being.

The science of being insofar as it is being can legitimately focus on form, or actuality, then, as the factor common to divine substances, matter-form compounds, and mathematical objects. But unless it can be shown that there is some explanatory connection between the forms in these different beings, the non-episodic nature of being itself will still not have been established, and the pictures given to us by the natural, mathematical, and theological sciences will, so to speak, be separate pictures, and the being they collectively portray, divided.

The next stage in the unification of being, and the legitimation of the science dealing with it insofar as it is being, is effected by an argument that trades, then, on the identification of form with actuality and matter with potentiality. And it is in *Metaphysics* Book XII Chapter 6 that the pertinent consequences are most decisively drawn:

> If there is something that is capable of moving things or acting on them, but that is not actively doing so, there will not [necessarily] be movement, since it is possible for what has a capacity not to activate it. There is no benefit, therefore, in positing eternal substances, as those who accept the Forms do, unless there is to be present in them some starting-point that is capable of causing change. Moreover, even this is not enough, and neither is another substance beyond the Forms. For if it will not be active, there will not be movement. Further, even if it will be active, it is not enough, if the substance of it is a capacity. For then there will not be *eternal* movement, since what is potentially

> may possibly not be. There must, therefore, be such a starting-point, the very substance of which is activity. Further, accordingly, these substances must be without matter. For they must be eternal, if indeed *anything* else is eternal. Therefore they must be activity. (*Met.* 1071^b12–22)

Matter-form compounds are, as such, capable of movement and change. The canonical examples of them—perhaps the only genuine or fully fledged ones—are living metabolizing beings (*Met.* 1041^b29–30). But if these beings are to be actual, there must be substances whose very essence is activity—substances that do not need to be activated by something else.

With matter-form compounds shown to be dependent on substantial activities for their actual being, a further element of vertical unification is introduced into beings, since layer-wise the two sorts of substances belong together. Laterally, though, disunity continues to threaten. For as yet nothing has been done to exclude the possibility that each compound substance has a distinct substantial activity as its own unique activator. Being, in that case, would be a set of ordered pairs, the first member of which was a substantial activity, the second a matter-form compound, with all its dependent attributes.

In *Metaphysics* Book XII Chapter 8 Aristotle initially takes a step in the direction of such a bipartite picture. He asks how many substantial activities are required to explain astronomical phenomena, such as the movements of the stars and planets, and answers that there must be forty-nine of them (1074[a]16). But these forty-nine are coordinated with each other so as to form a system. And what enables them to do so, and constitute a single heaven, is that there is a single prime mover of all of them:

> It is evident that there is but one heaven. For if there are many, as there are many human beings, the starting-point for each will be one in form but in number many. But all things that are many in number have matter, for one and the same account applies to many, for example, human beings, whereas Socrates is one. But the primary essence does not have matter, since it is an actuality. The primary immovable mover, therefore, is one both in account and in number. And so, therefore, is what is moved always and continuously. Therefore, there is only one heaven. (*Met.* 1074[a]31–38)

What accounts for the unity of the heaven, then, is that the movements in it are traceable back to a single cause—the prime or primary mover.

Leaving aside the question of just how this primary mover moves what it moves directly for the next section, the next phase in the unification of beings is the one in which the sublunary world is integrated with the already unified superlunary one studied by astronomy. This takes place in *Metaphysics* Book XII

Chapter 10. One obvious indication of this unification is the dependence of the reproductive cycles of plants and animals on the seasons, and their dependence, in turn, on the movements of the sun and moon (*Met.* 1071ᵃ13–16). And beyond even this there is the unity of the natural world itself, which is manifested in the ways in which its inhabitants are adapted to each other:

> All things are jointly organized in a way, although not in the same way—even swimming creatures, flying creatures, and plants. And the organization is not such that one thing has no relation to another but rather there is a relation. For all things are jointly organized in relation to one thing—but it is as in a household, where the free men least of all do things at random, but all or most of the things they do are organized, while the slaves and beasts can do a little for the common thing, but mostly do things at random. For this is the sort of starting-point that the nature is of each of them. I mean, for example, that all must at least come to be disaggregated [into their elements]; and similarly there are other things which they all share for the whole. (*Met.* 1075ᵃ16–25)

Thus the sublunary realm is sufficiently integrated with the superlunary one that we can speak of them as jointly having a nature and a ruler, and as being analogous to an army (1075ᵃ13) and a household (1075ᵃ22).

We may agree, then, that the divine substances in the superlunary realm and the compound substances in the sublunary one have prima facie been vertically integrated into a single explanatory system. When we look at the form of a sublunary matter-form compound, then, we will find in it the mark of a superlunary activator, just as we do in the case of the various heavenly bodies, and, as in the line of its efficient causes, we find "the sun and its movement in an inclined circle" (*Met.* 1071^{a}15–16). Still awaiting integration, though, are mathematical objects, such as numbers.

That there is mathematical structure present in the universe can seem to be especially clear in the case of the superlunary realm, just as mathematics itself, with its rigorous proofs and necessary and certain truths, can seem the very paradigm of scientific knowledge. So it is hardly surprising that some of Aristotle's predecessors, especially Pythagoreans and Platonists, thought that the primary causes and starting-points of beings are to be found in the part of reality that is mathematics friendly, or in some way mathematizable. For example, some Platonists (Plato among them, in Aristotle's much disputed view) held that for each sort of sublunary (or perceptible) thing there was an eternal intelligible Form or Idea to which it owed its being, and which owed its own being, in turn, to "the one," as its substance, and the so-called indefinite dyad of the great and the small, as its matter. So when we ask what makes a man a man, the answer will be, because it participates in the Form or Idea of a man, which owes its being to the way it is constructed or generated from the indefinite dyad and the one (*Ph.* 209^{b}7–16, 209^{b}33–210^{a}2). Because the Forms are so constructed, Aristotle says that "the Forms are numbers" (*Met.* 987b20–22). Between these Form numbers and the perceptible things are the ordinary numbers of mathematics, the so-called intermediates (*Met.* 987b14–15), which also depend on the Forms. In this elaborate system of, as I put it, mathematics-friendly objects, then, it is the Forms that are the substances—the ultimate starting-points and causes of beings insofar as they are beings.

Against these objects and the ontological role assigned to them, Aristotle launches a host of arguments (thirty-two or so in *Metaphysics* I 9 and many others elsewhere). In their place he proposes an entirely different account of mathematical objects, which treats them not as substantial starting-points and causes but as abstractions from perceptible sublunary beings—dependent entities, in other words, rather than separable or self-subsistent ones:

> The mathematician too busies himself about these things [planes, solids, lines, and points], although not insofar as each of them is the limit of a natural body, nor does he get a theoretical grasp on the coincidents of natural bodies insofar

> as they are such. That is why he separates them. For they are separable in the understanding from movement, and so their being separated makes no difference, nor does any falsehood result from it. (*Ph.* 193ᵇ31–35)

This completes the vertical and horizontal unification of being: attributes depend on substances, substantial matter-form compounds depend on substantial forms, or activities, numbers depend on matter-form compounds.

Beings are not said to be "in accord with one thing," then, as they would be if they formed a single first-order genus, but "with reference to one thing"—namely, a divine substance that is in essence an activity. And it is this more complex unity, compatible with generic diversity, and a genuine multiplicity of distinct first-order sciences, but just as robust and well grounded, that grounds and legitimates the science of being insofar as it is being as a single science dealing with a genuine object of study (*Met.* 1003ᵇ11–16). The long argument that leads to this conclusion is thus a sort of proof of the existence, and so of the possibility, of the science on which the *Metaphysics* focuses. It is also the justification for the claim, which we looked at before, that the science of being insofar as it is being is in fact theology (1026ᵃ27–32).

Dialectic and Scientific Starting-Points

If we think of a science in the exact sense as consisting exclusively of what is demonstrable, as we saw Aristotle himself sometimes does, we will be right to conclude that a treatise without demonstrations cannot be a scientific one—and this would include pretty much all of Aristotle's treatises, whether theoretical, practical (like the *Nicomachean Ethics* and *Politics*), or productive (like the *Topics* and *Rhetoric*). But if, as he also does, we include knowledge of starting-points as parts of science, we will not be right, since a treatise could contribute to a science not by demonstrating anything but by arguing to the starting-points themselves—an enterprise which could not without circularity consist of demonstrations *from* those starting-points: "For of a starting-point there is another sort of knowledge and not a demonstration" (*GA* 742^{b}32–33). Arguments leading from starting-points and arguments leading to starting-points are different, we are invited not to forget (*NE* 1095^{a}30–32), just as we are told that because establishing starting-points is "more than half the whole" (1098^{b}7), we should "make very serious efforts to define them correctly" (1098^{b}5–6). We might reasonably infer, therefore, that these Aristotelian treatises are contributions to science *at least in part* by establishing the correct definition of some of its starting-points.

Raw versus explanatory starting-points

Now in our investigation of starting-points, "we must," Aristotle says, "start from things known to us" (*NE* 1095^b3–4). That is why biology starts as it does: "First, then, we must grasp the parts of a human. For just as each group of people evaluates currency in relation to the one best known to themselves, it is the same way, of course, in other things. But of the animals the human is of necessity the best known to us" (*HA* 491^a19–23). For the sake of clarity, let us call these *raw starting-points*. These are the ones we start from when we are arguing to *explanatory scientific starting-points*. It is important not to confuse the two. In the case of the first-order sciences the *explanatory starting-points* include, in particular, definitions that specify the genus and differentiae of the real (as opposed to nominal) universal essences of the beings with which the science deals (*APo.* 93^b29–94^a19). That is why, a single science must deal with a single genus (87^a38–39)—or, as in the case of a higher-order science, something as empirically well-grounded as one.

To reach these definitions from *raw starting-points*, though, we first have to have the raw starting-points at hand. Aristotle is clear about this, as he is indeed about what is supposed to happen next:

The method (*hodos*) is the same in all cases, in philosophy as well as in the crafts or any sort of learning whatsoever. For one must observe for both terms what belongs to them and what they belong to, and be supplied with as many of these terms as possible, and one must investigate them by means of the three terms [in a syllogism], in one way when refuting, in another way when establishing something. When it is in accord with truth, it must be from the terms that are catalogued as truly belonging, but in dialectical deductions it must be from premises that are in accord with [reputable] belief. . . . Most of the starting-points, however, are special to each science. That is why experience must provide us with the starting-points where each is concerned—I mean, for example, that experience in astronomy must do so in the case of astronomical science. For when the things that appear to be so had been adequately grasped, the demonstrations in astronomy were found in the way we described. And it is the same way where any other craft or science whatsoever is concerned. Hence if what belongs to each thing has been grasped, at that point we can readily exhibit the demonstrations. For if nothing that truly belongs to the relevant things has been omitted from the collection, then concerning everything, if a demonstration of it exists we will be able to find it and give the demonstration, and if it is by nature indemonstrable, we will be able to make that evident. (*APr.* 46ᵃ3–27)

Once we have a catalogue of the *raw starting-points*, then, the demonstrative explanation of them from explanatory scientific starting-points is supposedly fairly routine. We should not, however, demand "the cause [or explanation] in all cases alike. Rather, in some it will be adequate if the fact that they are so has been correctly shown (*deiknunai*), as it is indeed where starting-points are concerned" (*NE* 1098ᵃ33–ᵇ2). But what exactly is it to show a starting-point correctly or adequately?

Here is Aristotle's answer:

> Dialectic is useful in the philosophical sciences because the capacity to go through the puzzles on both sides of a question will make it easier to discern what is true and what is false in each. Furthermore, dialectic is useful in relation to the primary [starting-points] in each science. For it is impossible to say anything about these based on the starting-points properly belonging to the science in question, since these starting-points are, of all of them, the primary ones, and it is through reputable beliefs (*endoxa*) about each that it is necessary to discuss them. This, though, is a task special to, or most characteristic of, dialectic. For because of its ability to stand outside and examine, it has a route toward the starting-points of all methods of inquiry. (*Top.* 101ᵃ34–ᵇ4)

And this is repeated almost word for word in the *Physics* with reference to the concept of place, which is a natural scientific starting-point:

> We must try to make our investigation in such a way that the what-it-is is given an account of, so that the puzzles are resolved, the things that are believed to belong to place will in fact belong to it, and furthermore, so that the cause of the difficulty and of the puzzles concerning it will be evident, since this is the best way of showing each thing. (*Ph.* 211^{a}7–11)

Prima facie, then, Aristotle's various treatises should correctly show explanatory starting-points by going through puzzles and solving these by appeal to reputable beliefs and perceptual evidence. But before we look to see whether that is what we do find, we need to be clearer about what exactly we should be looking for.

Dialectic is recognizably a descendant of the Socratic elenchus, which begins with a question like this: *Ti esti to agathon?* What is the good? The respondent, sometimes after a bit of nudging, comes up with a universal definition, what is good is what all the gods love, or whatever it might be (I adapt a well-known answer from Plato's *Euthyphro*). Socrates then puts this definition to the test by drawing attention to some things that seem true to the respondent himself but which conflict with his definition. The puzzle or *aporia* that results from this conflict then remains for the respondent to try to solve, usually by reformulating or rejecting his definition. Aristotle understood this process in terms that show its relationship to his own:

> Socrates, on the other hand, busied himself about the virtues of character, and in connection with them was the first to inquire about universal definition. . . . It was reasonable, though, that Socrates was inquiring about the what-it-is. For he was inquiring in order to deduce, and the what-it-is is a starting-point of deductions. For at that time there was not yet the strength in dialectic that enables people, and separately from the what-it-is, to investigate contraries, and whether the same science is a science of contraries. For there are two things that may be fairly ascribed to Socrates—inductive arguments and universal definition, both of which are concerned with a starting-point of scientific knowledge. (*Met.* 1078^{b}17–30)

In Plato too dialectic is primarily concerned with scientific starting-points, such as those of mathematics, and seems to consist in some sort of elenchus-like process of reformulating definitions in the face of conflicting evidence so as to render them puzzle free (*Republic* 532a–533d). Aristotle can reasonably be seen, then, as continuing this line of thought about dialectic.

Consider now the respondent's first answer, his first definition: what is good is what the gods love. Although it is soon shown to be incorrect, there is something quite remarkable about its very existence. Through experience shaped by acculturation and habituation involving the learning of a natural language, the respondent is confident that he can say what nobility is. He has learned to apply the word "good" to particular people, actions, and so on correctly enough to pass muster as knowing its meaning, knowing how to use it. From these particular cases he has reached a putative universal, something the particular cases have in common. But when he tries to define that universal in words, he gets it wrong, as Socrates shows. Here is Aristotle registering the significance of this: "The things that are knowable and primary for particular groups of people are often only slightly knowable and have little or nothing of the being in them. Nonetheless, beginning from things that are poorly known but known to ourselves, we must try to know the ones that are wholly knowable, proceeding, as has just been said, through the former" (*Met.* 1029^{b}8–12).

The route by which the respondent reaches the universal that he is unable to define correctly is what Aristotle calls induction (*epagôgê*). This begins with (1) perception of particulars, which leads to (2) retention of perceptual contents in memory, and, when many such contents have been retained, to (3) an experience, so that for the first time "there is a universal in the soul" (*APo.* 100^{a}3–16). The universal reached at stage (3), which is the one the respondent reaches, is described as "rather confused" and "more knowable by perception" (*Ph.* 184^{a}22–25).

It is the sort of universal, often quite complex, that constitutes a nominal essence corresponding to the nominal definition or meaning of a general term. Finally, (4) from experience come craft knowledge and scientific knowledge, when "from many intelligible objects arising from experience one universal supposition about similar objects is produced" (*Met.* 981ᵃ5–7).

The *nominal* (or meaning-based) definition of the general term "thunder," for example, might pick out the universal *loud noise in the clouds*. When science investigates the things that have this nominal essence, it may find that they also have a real essence or nature in terms of which their other features can be scientifically explained:

> Since a definition is said to be an account of what something is, it is evident that one sort will be an account of what its name, or some other name-like account, signifies—for example, what triangle signifies... Another sort of definition is an account that makes clear why it exists. So the former sort signifies something but does not show it, whereas the latter will evidently be like a demonstration of what it is, differing in arrangement from a demonstration. For there is a difference between saying why it thunders and saying what thunder is. In the first case you will say: because fire is being extinguished in the clouds. And what is thunder? The loud noise

> of fire being extinguished in the clouds. Hence the same account is given in different ways. In one way it is a continuous demonstration, in the other a definition. Further, a definition of thunder is a noise in the clouds, and this is a conclusion of the demonstration of what it is. The definition of an immediate item, though, is an indemonstrable positing (*thesis*) of what it is. (*APo*. 93ᵇ29–94ᵃ10)

A real (or synthetic, fact-based) definition, which analyzes this real essence into its "elements and starting-points" (*Ph*. 184ᵃ23), which will be definable but indemonstrable within the science, makes intrinsically clear what the nominal definition made clear only by enabling us to recognize instances of thunder in a fairly—but imperfectly—reliable way. As a result, thunder itself, now clearly a natural and not just a conventional kind, becomes better known not just to us but entirely or unconditionally. These analyzed universals, which are the sort reached at stage (4), are the ones suited to serve as starting-points of the sciences and crafts: "experienced people know the that but do not know the why, whereas craftsmen know the why, that is, the cause" (*Met*. 981ᵃ28–30). We might usefully think here of the definition of happiness, which is a starting-point of the practical science of ethics or politics, whose derivation we looked at in Chapter 4.

Dialectic and induction

Let us go back. We wanted to know what was involved in showing a scientific starting-point. We were told how we could *not* do this, namely, by demonstrating it from scientific starting-points. Next we learned that dialectic had a route to it from reputable beliefs. At the same time, we were told that induction had a route to it as well—something the *Nicomachean Ethics* also tells us: "we get a theoretical grasp of some starting-points through induction, some through perception, some through some sort of habituation, and others through other means" (1098^{b}3–4). This suggests that induction and dialectic are in some way or other related processes.

What shows a Socratic respondent to be wrong is an example that his definition does not fit. The presentation of the example might be quite indirect, however. It might take quite a bit of stage setting, elicited by the asking of many questions, to bring out a puzzle. But if it does succeed in doing so, it shows that the universal grasped by the respondent and the definition of it produced by him are not entirely or unconditionally knowable and that his state is not one of clear-eyed understanding:

> A puzzle in thought makes manifest a knot in the subject matter. For insofar as thought is puzzled it

> is like people who are tied up, since in both cases it is impossible to move forward. That is why we must get a theoretical grasp on all the difficulties beforehand, both for these reasons and because those who inquire without first going through the puzzles are like people who do not know where they have to go. And, in addition, a person [who has not already grasped the puzzles] does not even know whether he has found what he is inquiring into. For to someone like that the end is not clear, whereas to a person who has already grasped the puzzles it is clear. (*Met.* 995ᵃ30–ᵇ2)

But lack of such clear-eyed understanding of a scientific starting-point has serious downstream consequences:

> If we are to have scientific knowledge through demonstration, . . . we must know the starting-points better and be better persuaded of them than of what is being shown, but we must also not find anything more persuasive or better known among things opposed to the starting-points from which a contrary mistaken conclusion may be deduced, since someone who has unconditional scientific knowledge must be incapable of being persuaded out of it. (*APo.* 72ᵃ37–ᵇ4)

If dialectical examination brings to light a puzzle in a respondent's thought about a scientific starting-point, then, he cannot have any unconditional scientific knowledge even of what he may well be able to demonstrate correctly from it. Contrariwise, if dialectical examination brings to light no such puzzle, he apparently does have clear-eyed understanding, and his route to what he can demonstrate is free of obstacles.

The canonical occasion for the practice of the Socratic elenchus, obviously, is the examination of someone else. But there is nothing to prevent a person from practicing it on himself: "How could you think," Socrates asks Critias, "that I would refute you for any reason other than the one for which I would refute myself, fearing lest I might inadvertently think I know something when I don't know it?" (*Charmides* 166c–d). Dialectic is no different in this regard:

> But the philosopher, who is investigating by himself, does not care whether, though the things through which his deduction proceeds are true and knowable, the answerer does not concede them, because they are close to what was proposed at the start, and he foresees what is going to result, but rather is presumably eager for his claims to be as knowable and as close to it as possible. For it is from things of this sort that scientific deductions proceed. (*Top.* 155^{b}10–16)

What we are to imagine, then, is that the philosopher surveys the raw scientific starting-points, constructing detailed catalogues of these. He then tries to formulate definitions of the various universals involved in them that seem to be candidate scientific starting-points, testing these against the raw scientific starting-points by trying to construct demonstrations from them. But these definitions will often be no more than partial: the philosopher is only on his way to complete definitional starting-points, just as the demonstrations will often be no more than proto or nascent demonstrations. The often rudimentary demonstrations that we find in Aristotle's scientific treatises are surely parts of this process of arguing *to* not *from* starting-points. We argue to these in part by seeing whether or to what extent we could demonstrate from them.

Now, according to the official definition, reputable beliefs (*endoxa*) are "things that are believed by everyone, by the majority, or by the wise—either by all of them, or by most, or by the most well known and most reputable" (*Top*. 100^{b}21–23). Just as the scientist should have a catalogue of scientific (often perception-based) truths at hand from which to select the premises of his demonstrations, so a dialectician ought also to select premises "from arguments that have been written down and produce catalogues of them concerning each kind (*genos*) of subject, putting them under separate headings—for example, 'Concerned with good,' 'Concerned with life'" (105^{b}12–15). But for obvious reasons reputable beliefs in esoteric subjects like natural science (unlike, for example, ethics and politics) are likely to have predominantly expert rather than non-expert sources—although in Aristotle's world, as to some perhaps lesser extent in ours—everyone knows *something* about plants, animals, and so on. Thus the views that are reputable beliefs because they are those of other thinkers loom larger in some treatises than beliefs reputable because held by ordinary people rather than the wise. By the same token, things that appear to be so on the basis of observation should figure along with these beliefs (as at *Cael.* 303[a]22–23), since these, as we saw, have the controlling vote in natural science.

Clearly, then, there will be considerable overlap between the scientist's catalogue of raw starting-points and the honest dialectician's catalogue of reputable beliefs. For, first, things that are believed by reputably wise people are themselves reputable beliefs, and, second, any respondent would accept "the beliefs of those who have investigated the subjects in question—for example, on a question of medicine he will agree with a doctor, and on a question of geometry with a geometer" (*Top.* 104[a]8–37). The catalogues also differ, however, in that not all reputable beliefs need be true. If a proposition is a reputable belief, if it would be accepted by all or most people, it is everything an honest dialectician could ask for in a premise, since his goal is simply this: to show by honest deductions that a definition offered by any respondent whatsoever conflicts—if it does—with other beliefs the respondent has. That is why having a complete or fairly complete catalogue of reputable beliefs is such an important resource for a dialectician. It is because dialectic deals with things only "in relation to belief," then, and not as philosophy and science do, "in relation to truth" (105^b30–31), that it needs nothing more than reputable *beliefs*.

Nonetheless, the fact that all or most people believe something leads us "to trust it as something in accord with experience" (*Div. Somn.* 462^b14–16), and—since human beings "are naturally adequate as regards the truth and for the most part happen upon it" (*Rh.* 1355^a15–17)—as containing some truth. That is why having catalogued some of the things that people believe happiness to be, Aristotle writes: "Some of these views are held by many and are of long standing, while others are held by a few reputable men. And it is not reasonable to suppose that either group is entirely wrong, but rather that they are right on one point at least or even on most of them" (*NE* 1098^b27–29). Later he generalizes the claim: "things that seem to be so to everyone, these, we say, are" (1172^b36–1173^a1).

Raw starting-points are just that—raw. But when refined some shred of truth is likely to be found in them. So likely, indeed, that if none is found, this will itself be a surprising fact needing to be explained: "when a reasonable explanation is given of why an untrue view appears true, this makes us more convinced of the true view" (*NE* 1154^a24–25); "what we are about to say will also be more convincing to people who have previously heard the pleas of the arguments disputing them" (*Cael.* 279b7–9). It is the grain of truth enclosed in a reputable belief that a philosopher or scientist is interested in, then, not in the general acceptability of the surrounding husk, much of which he may discard.

The process of refinement in the case of a candidate explanatory starting-point is that of testing a definition of it against reputable beliefs and perceptual evidence. This may result in the definition being accepted as it stands or in its being altered or modified: when a definition is non-perspicuous, Aristotle tells us it must be "corrected and reconfigured" (*Top.* 151b7–8) until it is made clear. The same process applies to the reputable beliefs and perceptual evidence themselves, since they may conflict not only with the definition but also with each other. Again, this may result in their being modified, often by uncovering ambiguities within them or in the argument supporting them, or by drawing distinctions that uncover complexities in these, or they may be rejected entirely, provided that their appearance of truth is explained away.

The canonical occasion for the use of honest dialectic, as of the Socratic elenchus and plain dialectic, is of course the examination of someone else. The relevant premises for the questioner to use, therefore, are the reputable beliefs in his catalogue that his respondent will accept. Just how wide this set of beliefs is in a given case depends naturally on how accessible to untrained respondents the subject matter is on which he is being examined.

When a scientist is investigating by himself, the class of premises he will select from is the catalogue of *all* the raw starting-points of his science, despite a natural human inclination to do otherwise:

> [People] seem to inquire up to a certain point, but not as far as it is possible to take the puzzle. For it is customary for all of us to make our inquiry not with an eye to the thing at hand but with an eye to the person who says the contrary. For a person even inquires within himself up to the point at which he is no longer able to argue against himself. That is why a person who is going to inquire well must be capable of objecting by means of objections proper to the relevant genus, and this comes from having a theoretical grasp on all the differentiae. (*Cael.* 294b6–13)

It is a common complaint in *Generation of Animals* about previous thinkers that they have failed in this regard:

> Democritus made this error [about shedding of teeth], then, in speaking universally without investigating what happens in all cases. But this is what we must do. For it is necessary for the one who speaks universally to say something about all cases. (*GA* 788b17–20)

Hence a scientist will want to err on the side of excess, adding any reputable belief, any perceptual evidence, that appears to have any relevance whatsoever to his catalogue. When he formulates definitions of candidate scientific starting-points from which he thinks he can demonstrate the raw ones, he must then examine himself to see whether he really does have the scientific knowledge of it that he thinks he does. If he is investigating together with fellow scientists, others may examine him: we all do better with the aid of co-workers (*NE* 1177^{a}34). What he is doing is using honest dialectic on himself or having it used on him. But this, we see, is little different from the final stage of the induction we looked at earlier. Induction, as we might put it, is in its final stage (possibly self-directed) honest dialectic.

In a famous and much debated passage, Aristotle writes:

> We must, as in the other cases, set out the things that appear to be so, and first go through the puzzles, and, in that way, show preferably all the reputable beliefs about these ways of being affected, or, if not all of them, then most of them and the ones with the most authority. For if the objections are refuted and the reputable beliefs are left standing, that would be an adequate showing. (*NE* 1145^{b}2–7)

The specific topic of the comment is "these ways of being affected," which are self-control and its lack as well as resilience and softness. Some people think that it applies only to this topic and should not be generalized, even though "as in the other cases" surely suggests a wider scope. And, as we can now see that scope *is* in fact entirely general, since it describes the honest dialectical or inductive route to the starting-points of *all* the sciences and methods of inquiry, with "setting out the things that appear to be so" describing the initial phase in which the raw starting-points are collected and catalogued.

Dialectic and understanding

Now that we know what it means for dialectic as employed by the philosopher to provide a route to the explanatory starting-points of the sciences, we are in a position to see, if we look, that it is just such a route that most of Aristotle's treatises take. Since this route is the sort any science must take to show its explanatory starting-points, the investigation it undertakes is indeed a scientific one. It is not, to be sure, a demonstration from starting-points, but rather a showing of the starting-points themselves, which, if successful, allows us to achieve the sort of puzzle-free grasp on them that comes with genuine understanding. We might think of as the intellectual correlate of freeing the understanding of the burdens, associated with embodiment, that weigh it down, and that are responsible, in small children, for their top-heavy, dwarf-like appearance (*PA* 686^{a}25–687^{a}2).

God

At the end of Chapter 4 we saw that our happiness resides principally in contemplation, provided that our contemplation exemplifies the virtue of theoretical wisdom, and that it does so if we have scientific knowledge of what follows from scientific starting-points, understand the starting-points themselves, and our understanding and knowledge are of "the most estimable things" (*NE* 1141^{a}17–20). We now know what the first two require of us. But the third remains for us to explore more fully.

There, then, in the starry heavens above us, are the forty-nine celestial spheres, all of them alive, and moving eternally in fixed circular orbits. The outermost one, which contains all the others, is the primary heaven. Question: how is it moved by the primary mover, the primary god? Here is what Aristotle responds:

> [1] There is something [namely, the primary heaven,] that is always moved with an unceasing

movement, which is in a circle (and this is clear not from argument alone but also from the facts). So the primary heaven would be eternal. There is, therefore, also something that moves it [namely, the primary god]. But since what is moved and moves something is something medial, there is something that moves without being moved, being eternal, substance, and activity. This, though, is the way the object of desire and the intelligible object move things: they move them without being moved. Of these objects, the primary ones are the same. (*Met.* 1072^{a}21–27)

Thus the primary heaven is moved by the primary god, in the way that we are moved by a good that we desire. But how can the primary god be such a good? Moreover, why is he not moved by something else again?

The answer to the first of these questions is this:

[**2**] Active understanding, though, is intrinsically of what is intrinsically best, and the sort that is to the highest degree best is of what is to the highest degree best. The understanding actively understands itself by partaking of the intelligible object. (For it becomes an intelligible object by touching and understanding one, so that understanding and intelligible object are the same.) For what is receptive of the intelligible object and of the substance is the understanding, and it is active when it possesses it, so that this

rather than that seems to be the divine thing that understanding possesses, and contemplation seems to be most pleasant and best. **[3]** If, then, that good state [of activity], which we are sometimes in, the [primary] god is always in, that is a wonderful thing, and if to a higher degree, that is yet more wonderful. But that is his state. And life too certainly belongs to him. For the activity of understanding is life, and he is that activity; and his intrinsic activity is life that is best and eternal. (*Met.* 1072b18–28)

[1] reprises doctrines about the understanding that we have already worked through in Chapter 3, but **[3]** gives us the new information we need.

The desire that moves the heaven

What the primary heaven is moved by is the wish to be in the good state of active contemplation that we, when we are happiest, are in, and that the primary god is always in because he just is that activity. Just as we seek the good that the primary god is, so too does the primary heaven and its forty-eight celestial companions.

This brings us to our second question. When the understanding is actively contemplating something, that something—that intelligible object—is what activates it. So why isn't that object yet more primary than the primary god? The reasoning, though compressed, should now be fairly readily intelligible:

> [**4**] What does it [the primary god] understand? For it is either itself or something else. And if something else, then either always the same thing or sometimes this and sometimes that. Does it, then, make a difference or none at all whether it actively understands the good or some random object? Or are there not certain things that it would be absurd for it to think of? It is clear, therefore, that it actively understands what is most divine and most estimable and does not change [its object], since change would be for the worse, and would already be a sort of movement. First, then, if its substance is not active understanding but rather a capacity [to understand] … it is clear that something else would be more estimable than the understanding, namely, what is understood. And indeed [the capacity] to understand and active understanding will belong even to someone who actively understands the worst thing, so that if this is to be avoided (for there are in fact some things that it is better not to see than to see), the active understanding would not be the best thing. It is itself, therefore, that it understands, if indeed it is the most excellent thing, and the active understanding is active understanding of active understanding. (*Met.* $1074^{b}20$–35)

God understands himself, and is that understanding, because his understanding is like ours would be if we imagine it as being the intelligible equivalent of seeing light without seeing any other visible object. From the inside, then, from the point of view of the subject experiencing it, it is a state of consciousness of a sort familiar from the writings of the great religious mystics, in which both subject and object disappear from an awareness that yet remains fully and truly attentive, fully alive and joyous. Insofar as we have any experience-based evidence of what a beatific state is like, this one surely approximates to it. Were we to experience it or something like it, then, there is some reason to think that we would agree that it is bliss indeed, blessed happiness unalloyed.

Go back now to the *primacy dilemma* that we looked at earlier in this chapter and notice that its resolution is within our grasp, though one might be forgiven for not readily understanding Aristotle's statement of it:

> The fact that all scientific knowledge is universal, so that the starting-points of beings must also be universal and not separate substances, involves the greatest puzzle of those mentioned. But though there is surely a way in which what is said is true, there is another way in which it is not true. For scientific knowledge, like knowing scientifically, is twofold, one potential, the other active: the capacity [or potential], being as matter, universal and indefinite,

> is of what is universal and indefinite, whereas the activity, being definite, is of what is definite—being a this something of a this something. But it is only coincidentally that sight sees universal color, because this [particular instance of] color that it sees is a color, and so what the grammarian theoretically grasps, namely, this [particular instance of] A, is an A. For if the starting-points must be universal, what comes from them must also be universal, as in the case of demonstrations. And if this is so, there will be nothing separable and no substance either. However, in one way scientific knowledge is universal, but in another it is not. (*Met.* 1087ᵃ10–25)

The idea is this. In our passive understanding we have many forms or essences. Since these are universals, you may have the same ones in your passive understanding as I have in mine. For example, you and I both may understand the universal form or essence of the letter A. But when I actively contemplate—actively understand—that universal, what is now in my active understanding is a particular: this actualization of that universal. Now consider the primary god. He is eternally and essentially the object of the active understanding that he is. So he is a substantial particular, but since he is essentially an activity, he is also a universal essence of a special sort—one that can only be actual, never merely potential. In a way, then, the primary god overcomes the difference between particulars and universals that seemed unbridgeable. For he is at once a concrete particular and the starting-point of all scientific knowledge.

Let us quickly reprise the story in a sequence of texts. The first deals with the role of the understanding within us:

> A person is called "self-controlled" or "lacking in self-control" depending on whether or not his understanding is in control, on the supposition that this is what each person is, and it is actions involving reason that people seem most of all to do themselves and to do voluntarily. So it is clear enough that this part is what each person is or is most of all and that a decent person likes this part most. (*NE* 1168^b^34–1169^a^2)

The next analogizes the understanding's role in us to its role in the universe:

> What we are seeking is this: what the starting-point of movement in the soul is. And what it is, is clear. Just as in the whole [universe] the starting-point is god, so it is too in us. For the divine element in us in a way does all the moving. Of reason, however, the starting-point is not reason, but something superior. But what besides god is superior to both scientific knowledge and understanding, since virtue [of character] is an instrument of understanding? (*EE* 1248^a^24–29)

The next tells us how Aristotle's god is related to the good:

> Active understanding, though, is intrinsically of what is intrinsically best, and the sort that is to the highest degree best is of what is to the highest degree best…and contemplation seems to be most pleasant and best. If, then, that good state [of activity], which we are sometimes in, god is always in, that is a wonderful thing, and if to a higher degree, that is yet more wonderful. But that is his state. And life too certainly belongs to him. For the activity of understanding is life, and he is that activity; and his intrinsic activity is life that is best and eternal. (*Met.* XII 7 1072^b18–28)

The next draws the famous conclusion:

> It is itself, therefore, that [god] understands, if indeed it is the most excellent thing, and the active understanding is active understanding of active understanding. (*Met.* 1074^b33–35)

The next contrasts our understanding's grasp of the good with that of the primary god's:

> It is not in that way [namely, by understanding something else] that god is in the good state, rather, he is too good to understand anything besides himself, and the reason for this is that

> while the good for us has reference to something distinct, in his case he is his own good. (*EE* 1245b16–19)

Thus the primary god attains the good by understanding himself. We, on the other hand, attain it, not by reflexive self-understanding, but by understanding him.

On the role of understanding in the universe as a whole the next text is perhaps the most illuminating:

> One should think the action of the stars to be like that of animals and plants. For here [on earth] the actions of human beings are in fact most numerous, since it is possible to attain many goods, so that it is possible to do many things in action, and for the sake of other ones. (What is in the best state, by contrast, has no need of action, since it is itself the for-the-sake-of-which; action, though, is always in two [varieties], namely, when it is the for-the-sake-of-which and when it is what is for the sake of that.) The actions of the other animals, on the other hand, are fewer, and of the plants perhaps one small one. For either there is some one thing which they may attain, as there is for a human being too, or the many things are a route toward the best one. One thing, then, has and participates in the best, one reaches close to it by means of few [steps], another by means of many, and another does not even try, but it

is sufficient for it to come close to the ultimate [end]. For example, if health is the end, one thing, then, is always healthy, another is slimming down [to be healthy], another running and slimming down, another does some other action for the sake of running, so that its movements are more numerous; a distinct one, though, is incapable of reaching being healthy, but only of running or slimming down (and one or the other of these is the end for them). For on the one hand it is best of all for each to attain the [best] end; but on the other, if this is not [possible], it would always be better to the degree that it got closer to the best one. And this is why the earth does not move at all, and things close to it have few movements. For they do not reach the ultimate [end], but as far as is possible attain the most divine starting-point. The primary heaven, however, attains this directly by means of a single movement. But the bodies intermediate between the first and the last ones, though they do attain it, do so by means of more movements. (*Cael.* 292^{b}1–25)

What these texts tell us is that levels of happiness have to do with levels of grasp by understanding of the good, with the primary god, who *is* that good, having the highest level, the primary heaven the next, while on earth nothing has a higher level than that of the human being whose understanding grasps the good in active contemplation of it.

Contemplation and the need for social goods

Contemplation, however, is not something that we human beings are self-sufficient for: "To the extent that someone is a human being, he will also need external prosperity. For his nature is not self-sufficient for contemplation, but his body needs to be healthy and provided with food and other sorts of service" (*NE* 1178^b33–35). Included in the other sorts of service are a good upbringing, a good education, good scientific institutions, and, of course, the peace, tranquility, and leisure that contemplation requires. Consequently, these are things that must be provided by any society that aims to make its citizens happy.

Tired after a long day spent in un-leisurely activities, such as running the city or serving in the army, which are "accompanied by toil and strain" (*Pol.* 1337^b39–40), leisure first requires that we relax, and so we need something to relax us:

> "Amusing ourselves so as to engage in serious matters" … seems to be correct. For amusement is like relaxation, and it is because people cannot labor continuously that they need relaxation. Relaxation, then, is not an end. For it occurs for the sake of activity. (*NE* 1176^b33–1177^a1)

Thus the best city will "introduce amusement, but watch for the appropriate time to use it, as if dispensing it as a medicine [for the ills of unleisured work]" (*Pol.* 1337^{b}40–42). Once relaxed, we are ready for leisurely activities, which include playing and (especially) listening to music, which is for "passing the time in leisure" (1338^{a}21-22).

Beyond these not strictly contemplative activities, there are also a number of different contemplative ones:

> Of the substances composed by nature, some are un-generated and incapable of passing away for all eternity, while others participate in coming to be and passing away. But it has happened that where the former are concerned, though they are estimable and divine, our branches of theoretical knowledge are less developed (for both about the things on the basis of which one would investigate them and the things about them we long to know, the things evident to perception are altogether few). But where the plants and animals that are capable of passing away are concerned we are better equipped with a view to knowledge because of living together with them. For many things can be grasped about each genus if one wishes to take sufficient pains. Each of the two has its charms. For even if our contact with the eternal things is small, nonetheless because they are the most estimable ones knowing them is more pleasant than knowing all the things around

> us, just as a random small glimpse of the ones we love is a greater pleasure than seeing many other great things in exact detail. But because of knowing the others more and in greater number they take pre-eminence in scientific knowledge. Further, because they are nearer to us and more of our own nature, they provide some compensation in comparison to the philosophy concerned with divine things.... For even in the theoretical knowledge of animals disagreeable to perception, the nature that handicrafts them likewise provides enormous pleasures to those capable of knowing the causes by nature... That is why we must not be childishly disgusted at the investigation of the less estimable animals. For in all natural things there is something wondrous present. (*PA* $644^{b}21$–$645^{a}17$)

Of these, contemplation in accord with theoretical wisdom may be the one in which the best sort of happiness consists (*NE* $1178^{a}7$–8), but the others, as we see, have delights of their own to offer.

In fact, though it is seldom remarked on, the contemplation of god—at any rate when embodied human beings do it—seems itself positively to need these other delights:

> In no case, though, is the same thing always pleasant, because our nature is not simple but also has another element in it, in that we are mortals.

> As a result, if one of the two is doing something, it is contrary to the nature of our other nature, and when the two are equally balanced, what we are doing seems neither painful nor pleasant. For if the nature of some being were simple, the same action would always be most pleasant. That is why the god always enjoys a single simple pleasure. For there is not only an activity of moving but also an activity of unmoving, and pleasure is found more in rest than in movement. "Change in all things is sweet," as the poet says, because of a sort of wickedness. For just as a wicked human being is an easily changeable one, a nature that needs change is also wicked, since it is neither simple nor decent. (*NE* 1154^{b}20-31)

Contemplation of god may be the peak leisured activity, but human beings cannot stay on the peak for long, without needing to do something else. The happy life needs to be variegated, in other words, and cannot be monochrome, even if its one color is as dear to us as a loved one. Having climbed to the peak, and admired the view, we need to come back down.

Chapter 6
The Role of Ethics and Politics

Let us return now to the perceptual mean and to the image of an old-fashioned beam balance, or set of scales, of the sort that blind justice is often portrayed as holding. The very appearance of the balance seems to tell us what it is for it to be accurate. Our visual system, as we know from Chapter 3, is like such a balance. When we discriminate colors correctly it tilts just the right amount; when we discriminate them incorrectly, it tilts too much or too little. When it is generally in the first condition, so that we do discriminate colors correctly, it is in a perceptual mean. If each of our other perceptual capacities is in the mean relevant to it, they will all be good and accurate discriminators of colors, sounds, tastes, smells, and feels, as will the common sense in which those five small balances register their inputs. It is what constructs out of them a multi-sense picture of the three dimensional world of objects that are colored, make sounds, have tastes and smells, textures, and temperatures, occupy places, and trace out continuous spatiotemporal paths, as they move around causally interacting with each other and ourselves.

When we perceive white, and our perceptual system is in a mean, our perception is quite reliable, but when we perceive a coincidental perceptible (such as the son of Cleon), our perception may be erroneous. It is our perception of coincidental perceptibles, as we saw, that fear or some other appetite or feeling can distort, so that we may, even from a very slight resemblance, think that what we are seeing is our enemy, or, if we are in love, rather than in apparent danger, our beloved.

The perceptual mean and the virtuous mean

Our perceptual apparatus thus interacts with our motivational apparatus—with our appetites, feelings, and wishes. And it is this fact that brings the more familiar mean—the one we encounter in the *Nicomachean Ethics* in connection with the virtues of character—onto the scene.

Let us consider, for simplicity, just one such virtue, namely, courage (andreia). It is related to feelings of fear and confidence in the face of danger. Thus to be overly afraid of small dangers is to be cowardly, while to be overly confident in the face of large dangers is to be rash or foolhardy (*NE* 1107ᵃ33–ᵇ4). To be courageous, by contrast, is to have our fears in a mean, so that they measure dangers correctly, with the result that our feelings of fear, and the actions they cause and motivate, are correctly responsive to the dangers we face. Similar considerations apply to other feelings and actions. Thus temperance (*sôphrosunê*), for example, is concerned with the pleasures and pains of appetitive desires, such as those for food, drink, and sex (1107ᵇ4–8).

We may think of the virtues of character, then, as being, on the one hand, *filters*, since they filter out, or counteract, the distortions that our desires introduce into our perceptions, and, on the other hand, as being *lenses* that, now cleaned of distortions, reveal the world of values (at bottom, the world of pain producers and pleasure producers) to us, as it really is—as the perceptual mean reveals, for example, colors.

But the virtues of character are not enough by themselves to accomplish this task. In addition, we need the virtues of thought, or intellectual virtues: practical wisdom and theoretical wisdom. After all, to calibrate our desires, to set their balances in the right mean, we have to know what our good really is—and that involves knowing what we are and of what sort of world we are a part. For our good is the good of a certain (malleable within limits) animal in a (malleable within limits) natural environment.

A host of sciences (bodies of knowledge), both genuine and pretender, impinge on us and on our world: formal sciences (mathematics, logic, decision theory), natural sciences (physics, chemistry, biology, psychology), social sciences (economics), and so on. In the *Nicomachean Ethics* (1094^{a}6–^{b}7) Aristotle imagines all of these as organized into a pyramid, with politics, or political science, at the top, on the grounds that it is the science—the most architectonic, as he calls it—with the most control, the most authority. For it both decides which sciences should be part of a political community (part of the curriculum in a publicly-funded university, as we might say), who should study them and to what extent (who should be admitted to university and who should teach there), and how their diverse outputs should be employed to further the common good. In the *Politics* (1279^{a}25–31), indeed, Aristotle make it the very mark of a correct—as opposed to a deviant—political system, that its laws and everything else are organized so as to promote the common good of all its members, not that of the ruling class.

Returning to the virtues of character, let us think of them now as guardians of the soul, ensuring that we are free from enslavement to desires that at once distort our perception of the good (as revealed by the various sciences) and cause actions and behaviors that fail to embody that good. Suppose those guardians are in place. When we add the knowledge of what the good actually is, we now have not just the virtues of character but also the intellectual virtue of practical wisdom (*NE* 1144^{b}30–32). But practical wisdom, Aristotle tells us, is the same state of the soul as political science, differing from it only in its orientation: practical wisdom looks to the good of the individual; political science to the good of the city (1141^{b}23–24). But since human beings are by nature political animals (*Pol.* 1253^{a}2–3)—animals that do well in life only as part of a political community—the two orientations necessarily overlap.

Think now not about the enslavement to desires that distort our perception of values, but about the enslavement of our minds to experts and "influencers," which is just as big a problem. The virtues of character free us from the first, provided practical wisdom frees us from the second, but how—omniscience being humanly inaccessible—is it to do that? It is here that the well-educated person (*pepaideumenos*) enters the picture. He is someone who studies a subject not to acquire expert scientific knowledge of it but to become a discerning judge:

> Regarding every sort of theoretical knowledge and every methodical inquiry, the more humble and more estimable alike, there appear to be two

> ways for the state to be, one that may be well described as scientific knowledge of the subject matter, the other a certain sort of educatedness. For it is characteristic of a well-educated person to be able to judge accurately what is well said and what is not. For we consider someone who is well educated about the whole of things to be a person of this sort, and we think that being well educated consists in having the capacity to do what was just stated. But in one case, we consider a single individual to have the capacity to judge about (one might almost say) all things, in the other case, about a definite nature. For there might be another person with the same capacity as the one we have been discussing but about a part. So it is clear in the case of inquiry into nature too that there must be certain defining marks by reference to which we can appraise its way of showing things, separately from the question of what the truth is, whether thus or otherwise. (*PA* 639ᵃ1–15)

Thus a person well educated in medicine, for example, is capable of judging whether someone has treated a disease correctly (*Pol.* 1282ᵃ3–7), and the "unconditionally well-educated person," who is well educated in every subject or area, "seeks exactness in each area to the extent that the nature of its subject matter allows" (*NE* 1094ᵇ23–1095ᵃ2). We might think of the person who believes that if there is no algorithmic decision procedure in ethics, or no exceptionless moral truths, then there is no ethical knowledge, no right or wrong; or the person who expects from science the sort of infallibility that religion claims to provide; or the person who buys snake oil, or starts the latest diet, though neither has been scientifically tested. (Americans spend $8 billion on cosmetics each year and a staggering $30.2 billion on untested diet supplements, vitamins, and the rest!)

The most illuminating element in Aristotle's description of the well-educated person, however, is that he knows the defining marks by reference to which we can appraise a science's way of showing things, separately from the question of what the truth is, whether thus or otherwise—in other words, marks that enable us to determine whether a claimant to the title of the relevant science is the genuine article, without our having to know whether what it tells us is in fact true. The genuine sciences, after all, are our best routes to the truth. So our best route to which sciences are genuine cannot be through our science-independent knowledge of what the truth actually is. (Some religions deny this in some cases, of course, as do some political ideologies.)

Now in part on the basis of his own deep, often first-hand knowledge of the sciences of his day, Aristotle was confident that the sciences all employed the same basic explanatory notions, such as matter and form, potentiality and actuality. In an important sense, then, they all spoke the same language—a language that a well-educated person could himself learn. It was this, in part, that enabled him to see as a whole the world that each of the special sciences provides no more than a partial vision of, and to see himself and his place in it. Philosophy, in fact, in the form of the science of being insofar as it is being, is what provided this unified vision of self and world.

A major question for us, then, must be that of whether the idea of such a person—of an Aristotelian well-educated person—is any longer credible. And we might reasonably think that it is not. For disciplines have become so hyperspecialized, each with its own technical vocabulary, tools, explanatory strategies, standards of exactness and success, that it seems that no one, however well educated, could hope to have any worthwhile sort of understanding of all of them. We are and can only be, it seems, the slaves of experts—when, that is, we are not simply the slaves of some sort of ideological brain damage, whether peddled by a religion, a corporation, a political party, Fox News, or some favored blog or other (perhaps controlled by Russians)!

But before we succumb to despair, it is worth returning to Aristotle's idea of the pyramid of the sciences and to imagine enlarging it with *bridging skills* (to call them that), the aim of which is to transmit the knowledge of some science in a usable form to politicians and to citizens more generally. A good physics journalist (or physics popularizer) does this. It involves being able to read real physics and being able to talk to physicists not with the aim of doing physics oneself, but with the aim of being able to translate into "ordinary terms" what the physicist has to say in his technical and expert terms (terms that one must be an initiate in order to understand). Bridge-physics is a real skill and an immensely important one. Replace physics with climatology and bridge-physics with bridge-climatology and you can see why.

Philosophy surely has an important role to play here, by helping us to achieve some reasonably informed overall pictures of reality and our place in it, and some of the analytical skills needed to undermine false pictures. But since academic philosophy, somewhat to its shame, has become as fragmented and balkanized as the other sciences, what we would need, to continue the metaphor, is a *bridging philosophy*, informed by the specialized philosoph*ies*, and instilled with their respect for rigor and clarity, but more catholic in scope and intended audience, and so written in a language that any reasonably well educated person can understand and respond to with interest. Aristotle seems to have tried his hand at this sort of philosophy in some of his published works (of which only fragments remain), and to have succeeded rather well, since their prose, Cicero tells us, "flowed like a river of gold."

Aristotle arrived at his own great synthesis of theory and practice, as we saw, on empirical grounds, by reflecting on, and drawing inductive conclusions from, the various sciences as they existed in his day. He was not doing "armchair" philosophy, in other words, but rather drawing on his own vast knowledge of these sciences to reach a unified explanatory picture of being as such and our place in it as practical agents and theorizers. If we followed in his footsteps, drawing on *our* sciences, we would not, needless to say, reach his conclusions about the primary starting-points and causes of beings. If we are to be Aristotelians now it cannot be by parroting Aristotle's theories. But we would do well to take him as a paradigm of how we might be philosophers ourselves—a "paradigm in the heavens," so to speak, "for anyone who wishes to look at it and to found himself on the basis of what he sees" (Plato, *Republic* 592b).

Further Reading

The on-line *Stanford Encyclopedia of Philosophy* (http://plato.stanford.edu) has many excellent articles on Aristotle, with detailed bibliographies.

The following books are stimulating, accessible to non-specialists, and reliable:

Ackrill, J. L. (1981). *Aristotle the Philosopher.* Oxford University Press: Oxford

Lear, Jonathan (1988). *Aristotle: The Desire to Understand.* Cambridge University Press: Cambridge

Natali, Carlo (2013). *Aristotle: His Life and School.* Princeton University Press: Princeton.

Made in the USA
Middletown, DE
18 December 2023